Off With Their Wigs!

IMPRINT ACADEMIC

ia

Charles Banner is a Research Fellow at Policy Exchange. He read Classics at Lincoln College, Oxford, and Law at City University. He has worked in management consultancy and contributed to two Policy Exchange publications about the police in 2002. He teaches constitutional law at City University and is a part-time volunteer adviser in European Union and human rights law at the AIRE Centre in London. He is due to start work as a pupil barrister at Landmark Chambers in October 2004.

Alexander Deane is a Research Fellow at Policy Exchange. He read English Literature at Trinity College, Cambridge, International Relations at Griffith University, Australia, and Law at City University. He is a member of the British debating squad and the winner of several national debating competitions. He is due to begin work as a pupil barrister at 6 King's Bench Walk Chambers in October 2004.

Michael Beloff QC is a barrister and President of Trinity College, Oxford. He was called to the Bar in 1967 and became a QC in 1981. He has been a recorder and a deputy High Court judge and remains a judge of the Court of Appeal of Jersey and Guernsey. In 1986, he became the first Chairman of the Administrative Law Bar Association, of which he is now Vice-President. He has consistently been recognised in legal directories as one of the foremost QCs in several areas of law and is the author of numerous learned publications

Off With Their Wigs!
Judicial Revolution in Modern Britain

Charles Banner
and Alexander Deane

Foreword by
Hon. Michael Beloff QC

Published in the UK by Imprint Academic
PO Box 200, Exeter EX5 5YX, UK

Published in the USA by Imprint Academic
Philosophy Documentation Center
PO Box 7147, Charlottesville, VA 22906-7147, USA

ISBN 0 907845 843

Societas: Essays in political and cultural criticism
Volume 7

A CIP catalogue record for this book is available from the
British Library and US Library of Congress

Contents

Preface

On 12th June 2003, the Blair Government announced its intention to abolish the ancient office of Lord Chancellor and to establish a new Supreme Court to replace the Appellate Committee of the House of Lords as the highest court in the United Kingdom. Only it did not do so after consultation and open debate: these policies were put forward in the context of a Cabinet reshuffle.

Unfortunately, the Government's cavalier attitude to such important constitutional reforms meant that the principles underlying them were overshadowed by criticism of the way they in which were presented. This book aims to articulate and evaluate these principles. In recent years, a number of specialist legal publications have debated the merits of the law lords sitting in Parliament and of the Lord Chancellor combining the roles of Cabinet minister, judge, head of the judiciary and appointer of judges. We have tried to cover the subject in a manner that is more accessible to those without a background in law, whilst at the same time contributing to the academic debate by putting the arguments in the context of the Government's proposals for reform.

Our other principal aim is to examine the various alternative models for the new judicial infrastructure. During the summer of 2003, the Department for Constitutional Affairs published consultation papers on the features of the Supreme Court, the future of the judicial appointments process and the reallocation of the functions of the Lord Chancellor. This book forms Policy Exchange's reply: we have structured our chapters to mirror the three papers, offering detailed responses to the most important questions asked. We have also attempted to answer many key questions which the Government has regrettably passed over, such as whether it is time for a fully-blown Ministry of Justice. However, we do not cover all the issues raised by the consultation papers, since a number of them are too specialised and technical for a publication of this nature - for example, the process of granting litigants 'leave to appeal' to the highest court.

Given the Government's lack of consultation before announcing its proposals, we ourselves have interviewed a wide range of constitutional experts on the merits of reform and the various models for the new judicial infrastructure. Our discussions with them have formed the backbone of this book and are quoted at length throughout.

Most of our consultees were keen to talk about the future of the Queen's Counsel system, which the Government has also contemplated abolishing. Although not strictly a 'judicial' reform, this subject does interlink with that of judicial appointments: currently applicants for judicial office and for QC both depend upon the patronage of the Lord Chancellor, a Cabinet minister. Therefore, we have included a short chapter at the end of this book in response to the Government's consultation paper on Queen's Counsel.

We should like to thank all of our consultees for generously giving us their time and insight. Particular mention should be made of Michael Beloff QC, for adding weight to this book with his incisive foreword. We are also grateful to Richard Cornes, for clarifying some obscure points and providing us with his forthcoming article on this subject, Noel Worswick, for general guidance and advice, and Toby Boutle, for thoughtful comments on our early drafts. In addition, we owe thanks to John Schwartz for typesetting our manuscript and to our publishers, Imprint Academic, for their general support. In writing and researching what follows, Charles Banner had primary responsibility for Chapters 1-3; Alexander Deane for Chapters 4-5.

Charles Banner
Alexander Deane
6th October 2003

Consultees

We conducted 'on the record' interviews with the following constitutional and judicial experts during July, August and September 2003:

Robin Allen QC – practising barrister, recorder and Head of Chambers, Cloisters. Chairman of the Bar Conference in 2002 and of Bar in the Community from 2000 to 2002. Proposed a motion supporting the creation of a Supreme Court to a meeting of the Bar Council in June 2002.

Nicholas Barber – barrister and Senior Law Fellow of Trinity College, Oxford. Lecturer in constitutional law and theory at Oxford University.

Hon. Michael Beloff QC – practising barrister and President of Trinity College, Oxford. Formerly Head of Chambers, 4-5 Gray's Inn Square. Has held part-time judicial office as a recorder, deputy High Court judge and judge of the Court of Appeal of Jersey and Guernsey.

Ross Cranston QC MP – practising barrister, recorder and Labour MP for Dudley North. Solicitor General 1997-2001; previously Professor of

Commercial Law at the London School of Economics. Member of the Constitutional Affairs Select Committee (formerly the Select Committee on the Lord Chancellor's Department) since 2003.

Dr Christopher Forsyth – barrister and Fellow of Robinson College, Cambridge. Reader in Public Law and Director of the Centre for Public Law, University of Cambridge. Author of numerous learned publications, including the authoritative textbook, *Administrative Law* (with Prof. Sir William Wade).

Rt. Hon. Lord Justice Laws – Court of Appeal judge, formerly of the High Court. Author of several influential articles on constitutional law in learned journals.

Lord Lester of Herne Hill QC – practising barrister and Liberal Democrat peer. Leading proponent of reform of the Lord Chancellor and House of Lord Appellate Committee for many years. Former recorder and deputy High Court judge. Author of numerous learned articles on constitutional law and human rights. President of the Liberal Democrats Lawyers' Association and active legislator in the House of Lords.

Prof. Ian Loveland – practising barrister and Professor in Law at City University. Author of the leading textbook *Constitutional Law: A Critical Introduction* and other publications in public and comparative law.

Rt. Hon. Sir Nicholas Lyell QC – practising barrister and Conservative MP from 1979 to 2001. Former Attorney General (1992-1997), Solicitor General (1987-1992), and recorder. Chairman of the Society for Conservative Lawyers.

Dr Kate Malleson – Senior Lecturer in Law at the London School of Economics and leading authority in judicial studies. Member of the Joint Working Party on Equal Opportunities in Judicial Appointments, set up by the Lord Chancellor's Department. Her books include *The English Legal System* and *The New Judiciary*.

Robert Marshall-Andrews QC MP – practising barrister and Labour MP for Medway. Sits as a recorder and deputy High Court judge. Author of the novel *A Man Without Guilt*.

Roger Smith – Director of JUSTICE. Previously head of training and education at the Law Society, and Director of the Legal Action Group. *Note:* his observations to us were made in a personal capacity and do not necessarily represent the views of JUSTICE.

Paul Stinchcombe MP – barrister, specialising in public and planning law, and Labour MP for Wellingborough. Member of the Joint Committee on House of Lords Reform since 2003.

Kay Taylor – barrister and Parliamentary Legal Officer to Lord Lester of Herne Hill QC. Former Judicial Assistant to the Law Lords (assigned to Lord Steyn).

Andrew Tyrie MP – Conservative MP for Chichester. Former Fellow of Nuffield College, Oxford. Vice-Chair, All Party Parliamentary Group on Constitutional Reform. Long time supporter of democratic reform of the House of Lords and author of numerous pamphlets on constitutional reform.

In addition, 'off the record' interviews were held with a number of anonymous individuals in both private and public sectors.

Foreword

by Hon. Michael Beloff QC

I must declare an interest at the outset. I am in favour of the main thrust of the Government's trio of reforms, which the two Bright Young Things, authors of this provocative book, have described with a title part tabloid – part broadsheet. But I consider that the merits of the proposals were in inverse proportion to the merits of their presentation. The haste and secrecy with which the programme was announced was as unnecessary as it was counterproductive. Interest rate adjustment or invasion of enemy territory may require an element of surprise; constitutional change should be slow of gestation. If this was spin, then I can only conclude that the wicket was not turning.

But my support for the measures is conditioned by a sense of their inevitability, and accompanied by a soupçon of regret. All three seem to me to have a single source – the provision in Article 6 of the European Convention of Human Rights which makes mandatory an 'independent and impartial tribunal', reflecting the Roman law principle Nemo Judex in Causa Sua and Lord Hewart's oft misquoted dictum "Justice should not only be done but should manifestly and undoubtedly be seen to be done" (a competent sub-editor should have cut the adverbs). Neither a member of the executive (the Lord Chancellor) nor members of the legislature (the Law Lords) can on the basis of this rule be acceptable judges and – to revert to the tenant of the Woolsack – nor can he be the actual source of judicial appointment and preferment. If Westminster had not spoken sooner, Strasbourg could have done so later.

My regret is that the compelling case for change rests more in austere theory than in practical experience [although if the new Supreme Court is properly housed and provided for, and if the Secretary of State for Constitutional Affairs can become, as Lord Falconer intends, a deliverer of an effective legal system, tangible benefits will be the by-product of, if not the underlying motive for, the agenda].

The Lord Chancellor's judicial appointments have over the whole of my professional lifetime been of the highest calibre available to him; and the notion that politics nowadays enters the equation is exploded by Tory Lord Mackay's promotion of Stephen Sedley, a man of the left if ever there was one. The Law Lords' interventions in debates in the House have been pertinent. No one can identify any case where the content of the judicial decisions of either Lord Chancellor or Law Lords was actually affected adversely, indeed at all, by their triple or double roles, and virtually none where it might to the reasonable bystander have seemed so. Is it coincidence that the reputation of our highest judiciary is itself of the highest, away, it may perversely be, more than at home?

It is vital that the new system for judicial appointments, in my view, the key element of the package, be entirely free of the taint which is said to afflict the status quo. My espousal of a Commission in my Atkin Lecture in 1999 was a response to powerful cries by the Hague-led opposition for applicant-judges to be submitted to Parliamentary scrutiny in the manner of Supreme Court nominees in the USA. Quis custodiet ipsos custodies? In my view both the criteria for the Commission and the criteria for appointment to the bench should be written in statutory stone, and should emphasise the core values of impartiality and independence. The Commission cannot be or be seen to be the creature of the Government in power. Nor can it be permitted to succumb to the lures of political correctness: merit, not gender or racial diversity must be the touchstone of appointment. A seemingly two-tier judiciary within the same level in the judicial hierarchy would be destructive, not productive of justice.

And I believe too that the Chairman or Chairwoman must be a lawyer – why not the Lord Chief Justice? My service as Chairman of the Judicial Sub-Committee of the Senior Salaries Review Board convinced me that the advantages of insider knowledge outweigh the disadvantages of subconscious partisanship.

I have abstained from comment on the threat that hangs over the QC system, because my conflict of interest as commentator and silk is too palpable. The relevant proposal was Lord Irvine's last throw, not Lord Falconer's first. I content myself with observing that it was odd that no thought seems to have been given to the reaction of those countries in the Commonwealth that have continued to favour two ranks of Counsel, and I hope that their view will now be canvassed and paid heed to.

Modernisation is à la mode and the authors have vastly advanced the debate, with a judicious blend of "yes – if" as well as "yes – but". But some respect must be paid too to our national traditions. History after all is the major architect of constitutions: and unless we as citizens remember whence we came, we may not know whither we should go.

Michael J Beloff QC
President, Trinity College Oxford
of Blackstone Chambers, The Temple

1. Abolishing the House of Lords Appellate Committee

Introduction

It was surprising that the Government's intention to replace the Appellate Committee of the House of Lords with a new Supreme Court was announced in a press release principally concerned with a Cabinet reshuffle. Unlike the office of Lord Chancellor, the issue of the United Kingdom's highest court had nothing at all to do with a change-around in ministerial personnel. The proposed reforms were too fundamental to be mentioned as a footnote to the resignation of the Secretary of State for Health.

Moreover, it is regrettable that the Government did not see fit to consult as to the merits of taking the highest court out of Parliament before deciding upon such a proposal. The Department for Constitutional Affairs' 'consultation paper' on the Supreme Court was published a month after the announcement and only asked questions pertaining to the features of the new Supreme Court.[1] The changes

---

1   *Constitutional Reform: A Supreme Court for the United Kingdom* (Department for Constitutional Affairs, July 2003).

proposed are of huge constitutional importance and, as such, ought to have been the product of a wide, informed consensus rather than of party political machinations.

That being said, the idea of a Supreme Court has increasingly been the subject of public debate over the past decade. Two influential law lords, Lords Bingham and Steyn, have repeatedly called for their court to be removed from the legislature;[2] Le Sueur and Cornes produced a weighty paper in 2001 reaching a similar conclusion;[3] respected pressure groups such as the cross-party organisation JUSTICE have echoed their sentiments.[4] The issue has been debated in both Houses of Parliament in the context of the Blair Government's constitutional reform programme and has increasingly been the subject of lectures in the Inns of Court and at other academic institutions. To say that the proposed reforms have come totally out of the blue is off the mark.

What has suddenly shifted, however, is the Government's own policy on the issue. This appears largely to have been due to the particular personal views of Lord Chancellor Irvine, who vehemently opposed replacing the Appellate Committee with a new, institutionally separate court.[5] Since 1997, Lord Irvine had been in charge of co-ordinating the Government's constitutional reform programme, and until very recently appears to have been able to persuade the Prime Minister to follow his lead on the topic.[6] Consequently, *"over the past several years there have been a number of opportunities when reform could have*

---

2   See *eg.* Lord Steyn, *The Weakest and Least Dangerous Department of Government* [1997] P.L. 84; Lord Steyn, *The Case for a Supreme Court* (2002) 118 L.Q.R. 382; Lord Bingham, *The Evolving Constitution*, lecture to JUSTICE, October 2001.

3   Le Sueur and Cornes, *The Future of the United Kingdom's Highest Courts* (The Constitution Unit, 2001).

4   *Judicial Functions of the House of Lords*, written evidence to the Royal Commission on the Reform of the House of Lords (JUSTICE, May 1999); *A Supreme Court for the United Kingdom* (JUSTICE Policy Paper, November 2002); *A Supreme Court for the United Kingdom* (JUSTICE Briefing Paper, May 2003).

5   See *eg.* H.C. Debs., col. 155, 4 Dec 1998.

6   See *eg.* Nicholas Wyatt and Patrick Wintour, *PM Endorses Irvine on Lords*, The Guardian, 30th January 2002.

been considered, but was not."[7] No reference to the work of the law lords was included in the flagship White Paper *Modernising Justice* of December 1998.[8] The law lords' presence in the legislature was considered (and endorsed) by the Royal Commission on Reform of the House of Lords, but in a remarkably brief fashion[9] and principally from the perspective of what would be best from the House of Lords as a legislature, rather than what would be best for the Appellate Committee as a top court.[10]

So, far from being premature and/or inadequately discussed, the move to consider the position of the United Kingdom's highest courts is in fact well overdue. This was the view of Le Sueur and Cornes in 2001:

"It is something of a paradox that while being given important roles in the schemes to incorporate the ECHR into domestic law and in the devolution settlement, the Appellate Committee and the Judicial Committee have, as institutions, been so little affected by the forces of modernisation. They are instruments, but not subjects of change: new wine has been put into old bottles."[11]

Given this personal stranglehold Lord Irvine seems to have had on official government policy on administration of justice and constitutional reform, it is unsurprising that his removal from office has paved the way for a new line of thought on whether the Appellate Committee

---

7   Le Sueur & Cornes, *The Future of the United Kingdom's Highest Courts* (The Constitution Unit, 2001), p.48.

8   *Modernising Justice: The Government's Plans for Reforming Legal Services and the Courts* (Lord Chancellor's Department, December 1998).

9   See *A House for the Future. Royal Commission on the Reform of the House of Lords*, Cm. 4534 (January 2000), Chapter 9. Lord Steyn has said that the Commission was *"curiously truncated"* and *"avoided the searchlight being turned on...the merits of the idea of creating a Supreme Court"* [*The Case for a Supreme Court* (2002) 118 L.Q.R. 382 at p.390].

10   See Russell & Cornes, *The Royal Commission on Reform of the House of Lords: a House for the Future?* (2001) 82 M. L. R. 92.

11   Le Sueur & Cornes, *The Future of the United Kingdom's Highest Courts* (The Constitution Unit, 2001), p.142.

should be continued or replaced. It is just a shame that this new line of thought was brought to the fore in such a brash and haphazard manner.

The Appellate Committee of the House of Lords – an overview

The House of Lords hears appeals from the Court of Appeal in England and Wales, the Court of Appeal in Northern Ireland and – on civil matters only – the Scottish Court of Session. This jurisdiction has mediaeval origins,[12] but the system as we now know it is much younger. Up until the late nineteenth century, all lords could hear legal appeals, and the House itself was composed entirely of hereditary peers and bishops. In light of the increasingly apparent deficiencies of this system, the Appellate Jurisdiction Acts of 1876 and 1887 were passed in order to professionalize the House's judicial operations. This provided for judicially qualified life peers – the Lords of Appeal in Ordinary, or 'law lords' – specifically to be appointed to hear legal appeals. A further change was enacted in 1948, when the Appellate Committee was established so that hearings could take place outside of the Chamber, in a committee room in the Palace of Westminster. The law lords sit as full-time members of the Appellate Committee.

There are currently twelve law lords; the present convention is that two of these will come from Scotland and one from Northern Ireland. There is no equivalent convention in relation to Wales, its legal system being united with the English one. Any member of the House of Lords who has held 'high judicial office' is also eligible to sit;[13] this group, currently numbering fourteen, acts in practice as a reserve list for when

---

12 Its Scottish jurisdiction stems from the Treaty of Union in 1707 and its role at the apex of the English legal system traces back to the *curia Regis*, the Royal Council of English early mediaeval monarchs.

13 Appellate Jurisdiction Act 1876, s.5. 'High judicial office' includes the Appellate Committee, High Court, Court of Appeal and Court of Session, as well as the High Court and Court of Appeal of Northern Ireland.

full-time members are unavailable or when there is a requirement for one of the reserve members' particular expertise.

Cases are normally heard by panels of five law lords.[14] The appointment of twelve law lords means that, where possible, two panels can sit simultaneously. Although hearings usually take place in a committee room, each judgment is delivered in the Chamber of the House and formally exists as a report from the Appellate Committee to the House, to which the House has to agree. However, only the Appellate Committee members who are giving judgment speak and vote at sittings of the House for this purpose.

As life peers, the law lords are full members of the House of Lords and are able to take part in the legislative process – by speaking and voting in debates, and by chairing committees of the House.[15] They also sit with lay peers on the Committee for Privileges.

The Judicial Committee of the Privy Council – an overview

The Judicial Committee of the Privy Council, which also features prominently in the Government's proposals for reform, was established under the Judicial Committee Act 1833. Its membership is wider than that of the Appellate Committee; anyone who has held high judicial office and is a member of the Privy Council is eligible to sit. In practice, most cases are heard by law lords.

The Judicial Committee has three functions. Firstly, it is the final appeal court for a number of Commonwealth jurisdictions, overseas territories, Jersey, Guernsey and the Isle of Man. In these cases, the Judicial Committee sits as a court of the state concerned; its decisions are only of persuasive authority domestically. Secondly, under the Scotland Act 1998, the Northern Ireland Act 1998 and the Government

---

14   Cases of exceptional importance will be heard by larger panels, usually numbering seven.
15   In particular, Sub-committee E of the House of Lords European Committee and the Consolidation Bills Joint Committee.

of Wales Act 1998, the Judicial Committee hears cases where it is claimed that one of the devolved institutions has acted outside its powers. These are referred to it either from the courts in Scotland, Northern Ireland or England and Wales, or directly by the UK Government or one of the other devolved administrations. The Judicial Committee's decisions in these devolution cases are binding even upon the Appellate Committee.[16] Finally, the Judicial Committee has a limited ecclesiastical jurisdiction, under which only a very few cases are heard.[17]

The Case for Reform

At the time of going to press, the Government's proposals have only reached the consultation stage. Therefore, in this chapter we shall consider the merits of the decision to abolish the Appellate Committee, which has still to be debated and passed by both Houses of Parliament,[18] before moving on in Chapter Two to consider the various alternative models for a new, institutionally independent court.

At the outset, it should be noted that virtually none of the proponents of a Supreme Court are critics of the calibre, authority and probity of the individual law lords themselves. Lord Falconer, the new Secretary of State for Constitutional Affairs and Lord Chancellor, writes in his foreword to the Government's consultation paper:

"The decision does not imply any dissatisfaction with the performance of the House of Lords as our highest Court of Law. On the

---

16   See p. 59
17   Jurisdiction over appeals against decisions of governing bodies in certain healthcare professions are being transferred from the Privy Council to the High Court and Court of Session, under the NHS Reform and Health Care Professions Act 2002.
18   Because the Appellate Jurisdiction Acts 1876 and 1877 shall have to be repealed by an Act of Parliament.

contrary its judges have conducted themselves with the utmost integrity and independence."[19]

The case in favour of creating a new, institutionally independent Supreme Court is twofold. Firstly, the argument goes, the status of the country's highest court as a committee of its legislature is in principle undesirable. In an increasing number of cases, it may encourage legitimate doubts as to a law lord's impartiality and most likely breaches the United Kingdom's international human rights obligations; it runs contrary to the British constitutional principle of the rule of law, a corollary of which is a principle of 'separation of powers' strong enough to require judicial independence from the legislature; it engenders public confusion as to its true composition and as to the functions and powers of the different arms of the state. All these problems undermine public confidence in the judiciary – which, at only 59.5% is a whole 20% less than that in the United States[20] – and in the state as a whole, which is already at its lowest in living memory.[21] Furthermore, it leaves the British open to charges of hypocrisy on the world stage, where it is actively committed to promoting democracy, human rights, the rule of law and the separation of powers.

Secondly, it is said that the Appellate Committee's limited resources inside the Palace of Westminster, which cannot be improved due to lack of space, are seriously hampering the administration of justice.

Objective impartiality and Article 6(1) ECHR

There are several ways in which the courts interact with legislative

---

19   *Constitutional Reform: A Supreme Court for the United Kingdom* (Department for Constitutional Affairs, July 2003), p.4.

20   UK figure: average of four MORI polls, January 1999 – January 2002; US figure: MORI poll, November 1998.

21   As manifested, for example, in 2001 by the lowest General Election turnout since the universal franchise, with Pop Idol securing nearly twice as many votes amongst 18-24 year-olds (4.7 million to 8.7 million).

decisions and, in recent times, these have increased in both frequency and public profile. The courts have always had the final say on the interpretation of Acts of Parliament. On occasions, judges have seemingly contorted the meaning of a statute away from what the legislative majority appeared to have intended, in order to avoid a particularly offensive result.[22] Ten years ago, the landmark decision of *Pepper v Hart* rendered courts able, in certain circumstances, to examine the records of Parliamentary debates in order to clarify the meaning of an ambiguous statute.[23] Most recently, the Human Rights Act 1998 requires judges to construe Acts of Parliament, so far as possible, to be compatible with the European Convention on Human Rights, even where this involves straining the words of the statute.[24]

The ever-increasing importance and remit of judicial review – recently described by Lord Steyn as *"a foundation of our modern democracy"*[25] – also has implications for the relationship between the judiciary and the legislature. Whilst Acts of Parliament cannot be over-turned by the courts, the growing amount of delegated legislation, which is subject to approval and debate in the House of Commons and the House of Lords,[26] can be.[27] More generally, judicial review of decisions made by public bodies often involves matters of political controversy that have been or are the subject of Parliamentary debate.

The relationship between the judiciary and the legislature has been given a further twist as a result of our membership of the European Union and incorporation of the European Convention on Human Rights. Subject to the principle of Parliamentary supremacy, our courts

---

22   The most notable example is *Anisminic Ltd v Foreign Compensation Commission* [1969] 2 A.C. 147.
23   *Pepper (Inspector of Taxes) v Hart* [1993] A.C. 593.
24   Human Rights Act 1998, s.3.
25   Lord Steyn, *The Case for a Supreme Court* (2002) 118 L.Q.R. 382, at p.385.
26   For example, in 2000, the House of Lords rejected the Greater London Election Rules and a related order on election expenses because of a disagreement over granting candidates a free postal delivery.
27   See *Hoffman-La Roche v Trade Secretary* [1975] A.C. 295.

must now 'set aside' Acts of Parliament if they are inconsistent with directly effective EC law.[28] The Human Rights Act does not enable judges to overturn an Act of Parliament, but it does stipulate that a court may issue a 'declaration of incompatibility' whenever it finds a statutory provision to be incompatible with a Convention right.[29] So, even primary legislation is now subject to judicial scrutiny as to its substantive content.

In light of this increasing judicial interaction with legislative decisions, the objection has been made that the law lords' joint role as both legislators and judges may give rise to legitimate (even if in fact erroneous) doubts as to their impartiality in a growing number of cases. Lord Falconer himself stressed this argument when outlining the motives behind the Government's proposals for reform:

"We all recognise the dangers of judges perceived to have a view sympathetic to one side of the debate who then have to enforce the law.... Far better that the two roles are not confused."[30]

Like all other commentators on this issue, we do not question the integrity of the individual law lords in keeping separate their twin functions as judges and legislators. However, this is not enough to uphold the fundamental principle that, as Lord Hewart said in 1924, *"justice must not only be done but should manifestly and undoubtedly be seen to be done"* – in the eyes of litigants and the wider public. However scrupulous he may in fact be, a law lord's prior involvement in (for example) the passage of a piece of legislation may give the *appearance* that he is already committed to giving a particular judgment on future

---

28   *R v Secretary of State for Transport, ex parte Factortame (No 2)* [1991] 1 A.C. 603. A 'directly effective' EC provision is one which (according to ECJ jurisprudence) can be invoked in national courts.

29   Human Rights Act 1998, s.4.

30   Lord Falconer, Address to HM Judges, Mansion House, 9th July 2003.

cases concerning the interpretation or review of that legislation, regardless of the legal arguments before him. From an objective standpoint, he may not seem impartial.

The principle that justice must not only be done but should also be seen to be done is enshrined in Article 6(1) of the European Convention on Human Rights, which makes an *"independent and impartial tribunal"* the cornerstone of a fair trial.[31] The European Court of Human Rights has repeatedly made clear that this requirement is to be measured against objective, as well as subjective, standards:

> *"Under the objective test, it must be determined whether, quite apart from the judge's personal conduct, there are ascertainable facts which may raise doubts as to his impartiality. In this respect even appearances may be of a certain importance. What is at stake is the confidence which the courts in a democratic society must inspire in the public.... Accordingly, any judge in respect of whom there is a legitimate reason to fear a lack of impartiality must withdraw."*[32]

In other words, a court *"must offer sufficient guarantees to exclude any legitimate doubt"* as to its impartiality: a high burden of proof.[33] Following the coming into force of the Human Rights Act 1998, Article 6(1) is not only an international obligation of the United Kingdom, but it is part of our own domestic law.

Whether or not an overlap between judicial and legislative functions could result in a court lacking this 'objective impartiality' was the point at issue in two recent cases before the European Court of Human

---

31   For a detailed analysis of Article 6 ECHR, see Mole and Harby, *The Right to a Fair Trial* (Council of Europe, 2001). We owe a great deal to Nicholas Barber for enhancing our understanding of Article 6(1).

32   *Hauschildt v Denmark* (1989) 12 E. H. R. R. 266 at paragraph 47. See also (for example): *Piersack v Belgium*, (1982) 5 E. H. R. R. 169 at paragraph 30.

33   *Findlay v United Kingdom* [1997] 24 E. H. R. R. 221.

Rights. In *Procola v Luxembourg*, the Court examined the overlapping functions of the Judicial Committee of Luxembourg's Conseil d'État.[34] Four out of five members who sat as judges in an administrative law case had previously given a pre-legislative opinion on the legislative instrument which was the subject of that hearing. The European Court held that:

> *"The mere fact that certain persons successively performed these two types of function in respect of the same decisions is capable of casting doubt on the institution's structural impartiality."*[35]

Five years later, the overlapping roles of the Bailiff of Guernsey were challenged in *McGonnell v United Kingdom*.[36] The Bailiff had presided over the hearing of Mr McGonnell's planning appeal in 1995 (a judicial function), as well as presiding as Deputy-Bailiff in 1990 over the passage of the island's development plan (a legislative function), on which the decision to refuse Mr McGonnell's planning appeal had been based.[37] The Court held:

> *"Any direct involvement in the passage of legislation, or of executive rules, is likely to be sufficient to cast doubt on the judicial impartiality of a person subsequently called to determine a dispute over whether reasons exist to permit a variation from the wording of the legislation or rules at issue."*[38]

The mere fact that the Bailiff had presided over the legislature when it was debating and passing the legislation which the Bailiff later took

---

34   *Procola v Luxembourg* (1995) 2 E. H. R. R. 193.
35   At paragraph 45.
36   *McGonnell v United Kingdom* (2000) 30 E. H. R. R. 289.
37   As head of the Island's administration, the Bailiff was also a senior executive officer.
38   At paragraph 55.

part in interpreting was *"capable of casting doubt on his impartiality"* – consequently, Article 6(1) was breached.[39]

Attempts might be made to distinguish this case from the position of the Appellate Committee on three grounds: unlike the Bailiff, the law lords have no executive role; they do not *preside* over the legislative process; the executive and judiciary in Guernsey are so small that the Bailiff's overlap was accentuated. However, an influential article by Richard Cornes has outlined how each of these arguments is weak.[40] The first ignores the judgment in *Procola*, which concerned an overlap between only judicial and legislative functions.[41] As for the second, the Bailiff's position as a presiding officer is in fact a lesser overlap than that of the law lords. A presiding officer expresses no view on a legislative proposal (unless called upon to exercise a casting vote), whereas a law lord necessarily expresses a view on a piece of legislation if he speaks or votes on it.[42] Thirdly, whilst in an overwhelming numerical minority amongst the legislature, the law lords' opinions on legal matters will be given greater weight in Parliament *because* of their judicial role. Their position is thus comparable to that of the Bailiff and vulnerable to a legal challenge.

> "Once the wave of history has swept the Bailiff of Guernsey out of the ocean, it's but a matter of time before the tide comes up the Thames and sweeps through the apartments of the House of Lords" – **Roger Smith**

The implications of Article 6(1) ECHR, in light of this case law from European Court of Human Rights and the United Kingdom's incorporation of the Convention into domestic law in 2000, are recognised in

---

39   At paragraph 57.
40   Cornes, *McGonnell v United Kingdom, the Lord Chancellor and the Law Lords*, [2000] P.L. 166.
41   See p.29
42   Cornes, *McGonnell v United Kingdom, the Lord Chancellor and the Law Lords*, [2000] P.L. 166, at p.172.

the preface to the latest edition of the authoritative textbook on public law in England and Wales:

"Any mixture of judicial with legislative or executive functions... is now likely to prove vulnerable."[43]

As to the extent of the problem, the Court in *McGonnell* made clear that Article 6(1) does not require a strict institutional separation of powers between the legislature and the judiciary.[44] Rather, each case must now be assessed on its merits.

"The question must be asked on a case by case basis whether, for example, a law lord's prior participation in legislative debate on a provision now before him in a judicial setting, means he cannot be viewed as impartial."[45]

However, the aforementioned increasing judicial interaction with legislative decisions has correspondingly multiplied the potential frequency for such challenges to the Appellate Committee. The inevitability of the problem was highlighted, a year after *McGonnell*, at a session of the Joint Committee on Human Rights.[46] Asked by Sir Patrick Cormack MP as to whether Article 6(1) ECHR and the law lords' dual functions as judges and legislators were compatible, Lord Bingham and Lord Phillips MR declined to comment. Lord Bingham explained:

"I am afraid I see this as a question that will become litigious at some

---

43   Wade and Forsyth, *Administrative Law* (Oxford University Press, 2000), preface.
44   This was recently restated by the ECtHR in the case of *Kleyn v Netherlands*, 6th May 2003, unreported.
45   Cornes, *McGonnell v United Kingdom, the Lord Chancellor and the Law Lords*, [2000] P.L. 166 at p.172.
46   Minutes of Evidence, 26th March 2001.

point and therefore I would not like to give any answer to the question here and now."

The Royal Commission on Reform of the House of Lords – which in passing rejected calls for the abolition of the Appellate Committee whilst acknowledging that the issue was outside its remit – did not address the potential implications of *McGonnell v UK* for the law lords, noting the decision as of relevance only to the position of the Lord Chancellor.[47] Notwithstanding this, it did observe that overly partisan interventions by the law lords in their legislative capacity could call into question the appropriateness of a law lord sitting in any subsequent case involving the statute in respect of which he had some legislative involvement, and suggested that the law lords should clarify the basis on which they would take part in legislative matters in future.[48] The law lords followed this recommendation and agreed upon the terms of a practice statement which the Senior Law Lord, Lord Bingham, read to the house in June 2000:

"First, the Lords of Appeal in Ordinary do not think it appropriate to engage in matters where there is a strong element of party political controversy; and secondly, the Lords of Appeal in Ordinary bear in mind that they might render themselves ineligible to sit judicially if they were to express an opinion on a matter which might later be relevant to an appeal to the House. The Lords of Appeal in Ordinary will continue to be guided by these broad principles. They stress that it is impossible to frame rules which cover every eventuality. In the end it must be for the judgment of each individual Lord of Appeal to decide how to conduct himself in any particular situation."[49]

---

47   See Le Sueur & Cornes, *The Future of the United Kingdom's Highest Courts* (The Constitution Unit, 2001), p.142.

48   *A House for the Future*, Cm. 4534 (HMSO, 2000), chapter 9.

49   H.L. Debs., col. 419, 22 June 2000.

Whilst limiting the scope for judicial decisions by the law lords being challenged under Article 6(1), Lord Bingham's practice statement effectively removed the strongest argument for keeping judges of the highest court within the legislature: that they provided Parliament with a wealth of expert advice on legal issues.[50]

Moreover, questions remain as to whether the practice statement was enough to ensure that, in all subsequent cases, the law lords' dual functions could never compromise their objective impartiality. The statement has no force: it is clear from the wording that its contents are no more than discretionary guidelines. Law Lords have continued occasionally to speak in controversial debates on subjects of potential litigation. For example, Lord Scott of Foscote spoke passionately in opposition to the Hunting Bill in 2001, concluding:

> *"To impose the ban would be a misuse of law.... It would be profoundly undemocratic.... Democracy requires respect for the rights, beliefs and traditions of the minority. That would be offended if the Bill became law."*[51]

Even if all future law lords *were* strictly to follow Lord Bingham's practice statement, instances can be conceived where objective impartiality in a particular case may be compromised by a law lord's position in Parliament. Legislative functions of the law lords which remain untouched by the practice statement include chairing Committees of the House[52] and (when necessary) hearing pre-legislative references under the Scotland, Government of Wales, or Northern Ireland Acts of

---

50   See pp 46–47.
51   H.L. Debs., col. 649, 12 March 2001. Had that Bill become law and a 'declaration of incompatibility' sought in the courts under s.4 of the Human Rights Act 1998, would an affirmative judgment by Lord Scott have survived an Article 6(1) challenge?
52   In particular, the Consolidation Bills Joint Committee and Sub-committee E of the House of Lords European Committee, which, as Lord Lester of Herne Hill QC told us from his personal experience of sitting upon it, is often the forum for matters of marked political controversy.

1998.[53] Even where he has exercised neither his speaking nor his voting rights, a law lord may still be overly exposed to one side of a potentially litigious issue through being lobbied. For example, at the same time as the Appellate Committee was hearing a recent case concerning a legislative provision regulating covert policing, a Bill on the issue was before the legislative Chamber of the House of Lords;[54] during a recess in the judicial hearing, one of the judges was lobbied by a pressure group inviting him, in his legislative capacity, to intervene in Parliamentary debate on the proposed reforms.[55] So, the scope remains for the law lords' dual role as judges and legislators to fall foul of Article 6(1) ECHR in certain cases. To see Lord Bingham's practice statement as the end of the problem is, as the leading article on *McGonnell* concluded, *"overly optimistic."*[56]

Furthermore, the European Union's Charter of Fundamental Rights, which seems likely to become binding upon EU Member States upon the adoption of the EU Constitution in 2004, may also be breached in the circumstances outlined above. Article 47, like Article 6(1) of the ECHR, provides for an *"independent and impartial tribunal"*; it would be far from unsurprising if the European Court of Justice chose to interpret this requirement in the same way as the European Court of Human Rights has interpreted Article 6(1).

Those who are sceptical of the merits of the European Convention on Human Rights and/or the European Union might claim that all of this should be irrelevant to our own domestic system. Others might favour a different, less stringent interpretation of Article 6(1).[57] To such

---

53   It should be remembered that it was a pre-legislative reference, not a speech in a Parliamentary debate, which constituted the offending overlap in *Procola v Luxembourg*. See p.29.

54   Out of respect for the judge involved, we have not named this case.

55   See *A Supreme Court for the United Kingdom* (JUSTICE Briefing Paper, May 2003). The story was initially told by Vera Baird QC MP at a Charter 88 meeting on 15th May 2002.

56   Cornes, *McGonnell v United Kingdom, the Lord Chancellor and the Law Lords*, [2000] P.L. 166, at p.176.

57   For example, the separate concurring speech of Sir John Laws (sitting as an *ad hoc* judge) in *McGonnell v UK*. His version of the test appears less stringent than that put forward by the European Court in this case and on the previous occasions cited above. See Cornes, *McGonnell v United Kingdom, the Lord Chancellor and the Law Lords*, [2000] P.L. 166, at p. 173.

people, we emphasise that the principle upheld by the European Court in these Article 6(1) cases is important not merely because of its status as Convention right.[58] Public confidence in the justice system depends upon public *perceptions* of it – rather than the reality. It is therefore fundamental that judges are seen to be impartial. The European Court is right to impose a high burden upon the court's objective impartiality – there must be *no legitimate doubts* – for even the slightest reasonable suspicion of partiality in the highest court is capable of haemorrhaging public confidence in the justice system, especially in these days of increasing media scrutiny of the top courts' judgments.[59] It is a short step from lack of confidence in the justice system to general disrespect for the law and the state, which, even in small sections of society, has highly damaging practical implications.

The rule of law and the separation of powers

Unlike some other nations – most famously, the United States – Britain does not have an *institutional* separation of powers that can be invoked in its own right as a constitutional principle in favour of removing the highest court from the legislature. But that is not to say that 'separation of powers' is not a British constitutional principle at all, or that it is irrelevant to this debate. Rather, it is in large part a corollary of other overarching British constitutional principles – in particular, the rule of law.[60]

On any interpretation, the rule of law stipulates that the executive must act within the bounds granted to it under statute and the common law, which must in turn be decided by a judiciary inde-

---

58   Which itself does mean that the United Kingdom is obliged to uphold Article 6(1) (the same is likely soon to be true of Article 47 of the EU Charter of Fundamental Rights).

59   Prompted by interest in the enactment of the Human Rights Act 1998 and the *Pinochet* case (on which, see *e.g.* Harrison, *What Pinochet Has Done for the Law Lords*, (1999) 149 *New Law Journal* 477).

60   For the rule of law as a British constitutional principle, see Turpin, *British Government and the Constitution* (3rd edn., Butterworths, 1999); Jowell and Oliver (eds.), *The Changing Constitution* (3rd edn., Clarendon Press, 1994).

pendent of the executive.[61] Hence the 'separation' between executive and legislature, and judiciary and executive.[62] This is particularly problematic for the position of the Lord Chancellor, as discussed in Chapter Three.[63]

However, as Robin Allen QC emphasised to us, the legislature is also subject to the rule of law.[64] Underpinning the principle that the executive does not itself hold legal power is the notion that the exercise of arbitrary power is undesirable.[65] Therefore, it is inconsistent with the rule of law for legislature to grant the executive any arbitrary powers – to take an extreme example, a statute permitting the Home Secretary to imprison anyone he likes, whenever he likes, for whatever reason he would like would contravene this principle. *"Parliament is not the source of the rule of law; it works within the context of the rule of law."*[66] Although Parliamentary supremacy means that the courts cannot overturn an Act of Parliament for such a contravention, they have other methods in their ammunition, such as statutory interpretation:

"Unless there is the clearest provision to the contrary, Parliament must be presumed not to legislate contrary to the rule of law."[67]

---

61   See McEldowney, *Dicey in Historical Perspective*, in McAulsan and McEldowney (eds.), *Law, Legitimacy and the Constitution* (Sweet and Maxwell, 1985), p.188. Some, more controversial, interpretations view the rule of law as embodying this and various other more material rights [see: Craig, *Formal and Substantive Conceptions of the Rule of Law* (1997) P.L. 467; Wade and Forsyth, *Administrative Law* (Oxford University Press, 2000), pp.21-23 and especially p.23].

62   Cases in which senior judges have acknowledged this conception of 'separation of powers' include: *Hinds v The Queen* [1977] A.C. 195; *Duport Steels Ltd v Sirs* [1980] 1 WLR 142; *M v Home Office* [1994] 1 A.C. 377; *R v Secretary of State for the Home Department ex parte Fire Brigades Union* [1995] 2 WLR 1 per Sir Thomas Bingham MR at p.8 (CA) and [1995] 2 A.C. 513, per Lord Mustill at p.567 (HL).

63   See p.89.

64   Even on the orthodox Diceyian interpretation: see note 61, above.

65   Dicey himself defined the rule of law as *"the absolute supremacy or predominance of regular law as opposed to the influence of arbitrary power."*

66   Robin Allen QC.

67   *R v Home Secretary, ex parte Pierson* [1998] A.C. 539 at 591, per Lord Steyn.

If the courts' role as protectors against executive inroads into the rule of law requires judicial independence from the executive, then it follows that their corresponding role against similar inroads by the legislature requires judges to be independent from that arm of the state as well. To that extent, the 'separation of powers' may be invoked as a British constitutional principle in favour of removing the highest court from the shadow of the legislature. Given the executive's ever-greater control over the legislature and the courts' increasing interaction with legislative decisions,[68] this argument for 'separation' of the judiciary from the legislature can no longer be treated as an irrelevant theoretical issue.

> "The purpose of a judiciary separate from the legislature is, once the laws have been made, to give them life in the context of the rule of law." – **Robin Allen QC**

This problem is not sufficiently rebutted by the argument that the personal integrity of the individual law lords should ensure that, in reality, they are intellectually independent from the legislature. Again, perception is crucial. To quote Lord Steyn:

> *"It is of paramount importance that the nation must have confidence in judges at every level as independent and impartial guardians of the rule of law."*[69]

If the judges are not *seen* to be independent guardians of the rule of law against intrusions by any other arm of the state, including the legislature, what is the public to make of the judiciary and the state as a whole?

Failing to lead by example?
A practical and contemporary problem which, it has been argued,

---

68   See pp. 25–27
69   Lord Steyn, *The Case for a Supreme Court*, (2002) 118 L.Q.R. 382, at p.389.

stems from this failure of our legal system to adhere to these basic conceptions of the rule of law and separation of powers, is that Britain opens itself up to charges of not practising at home what it preaches on the world stage.[70] In an age when we actively promote democracy, human rights, the rule of law and even the separation of powers across the globe, the existence of our highest court as a sub-committee of our legislature – found in no other democracy – is a hypocrisy. Conversely, it is said that an institutionally independent Supreme Court *"would be a potent symbol of the allegiance of our country to the rule of law."*[71] Lord Falconer himself has cited this as a key motive for reform:

> *"We cannot allow in our courts what we would condemn in the courts of other countries.... It is no longer possible to say one thing to others about the separation of powers and do another at home."*[72]

A number of our interviewees saw this as a valid (albeit not decisive) point. We are inclined to agree. The 'rule of law' was repeatedly invoked by Tony Blair in foreign policy speeches advocating the recent military action against Iraq. Abdul Salam Azimi, the Vice-Chairman of post-Taleban Afghanistan's Constitutional Commission, has said that the new Afghanistan Constitution will include *"a separation of powers between the executive, the legislature and the judiciary"* and in doing so will reflect and be influenced by *"international norms."*[73]

The contradiction between what we advise and help to implement in other nations and our own institutional overlap has not gone unnoticed abroad. Dr Christopher Forsyth recounted to us how, when lecturing abroad on constitutional principles, he would emphasise how important the doctrine of separation of powers was against arbitrary power, only

---

70   See Lord Steyn, *The Case for a Supreme Court*, (2002) 118 L.Q.R. 382, at p.383.
71   Lord Steyn, *The Case for a Supreme Court*, (2002) 118 L.Q.R. 382, at p.384.
72   Lord Falconer, Address to HM Judges, Mansion House, 9th July 2003.
73   Source: UN OCHA Integrated Regional Information Network, 2nd June 2003.

for his audience to throw the examples of the law lords and Lord Chancellor back at him: *"it was an embarrassment to have to explain."*

Moreover, nationals of foreign countries without a detailed knowledge of the British constitution may also think that the overlap between the judiciary and the legislature is more far-reaching than it in fact is. As Lord Bingham observed in 2001, when the famous *Pinochet No. 1* case came before the law lords,[74] foreign observers mistakenly thought that the issue at stake had become political rather than judicial.[75] Lord Steyn, too, has observed that, when the judges gave their decisions in that case, following the protocol that judgments are delivered in the Chamber of the House of Lords and must be voted upon by the House:[76]

"...the crowded benches of the Chamber apparently led foreign television viewers to believe that Lady Thatcher was part of the dissenting minority who opposed the extradition of General Pinochet!"[77]

Such perceptions, however misguided, are inevitable under the current system; they can only fuel perceptions of Britain as hypocritical in its global support for democracy, human rights, the rule of law and the separation of powers. On its own, this point may not be enough to justify reform; nonetheless, it adds considerable ballast to the other arguments for change.

Constitutional clarification

Another wide-ranging criticism of the current system is that it engenders public confusion not just abroad but (arguably more

---

74   *R v Bow Street Metropolitan Stipendiary Magistrate, ex parte Pinochet Ugarte* [2000] 1 A.C. 61.

75   Lord Bingham, *The Evolving Constitution*, lecture to JUSTICE, October 2001.

76   Although the reality is that, in practice, only members of the Committee who are giving judgment speak and vote at sittings of the House for this purpose. See p.23.

77   Lord Steyn, *The Case for a Supreme Court*, (2002) 118 L.Q.R. 382 at p.382.

importantly) amongst British citizens as to the functions and powers of the different institutions of government. As Walter Bagehot said in 1867:

> "The supreme court of the English people ought to be a great conspic-
> uous tribunal... [; it] ought not to be hidden beneath the robes of a
> legislative assembly."[78]

Some people may not be able to see behind these robes; it may not be immediately clear that final legal appeals in this country are not heard by the House of Lords *as a whole*. This is made all the more likely by the procedure that judgments of the Appellate Committee are delivered in the Chamber of the House and the House then has to agree to them.[79] Furthermore, according to convention, at least one case per year is actually *heard* in the Chamber. Robin Allen QC told us of his first-hand experience of this in the employment law case of *Polkey v AE Dayton Services Ltd*:[80]

> "My client, who won, was absolutely delighted to have his case heard
> in the House of Lords. He was a simple, ordinary man from
> Nottingham who had known nothing in his life like this, loved every
> minute of this, and was certainly totally convinced in the end that
> Parliament had spoken in his case."

General public confusion over the basic nature and powers of funda-mental state institutions such as the courts and Parliament can sap away at public confidence in them. A recent empirical study has shown that two of the most common criticisms of the judiciary are inaccessibility and lack

---

78   Bagehot, *The English Constitution* (Fontana Press, 1993), p.149.
79   See note 76, above.
80   [1988] 1 A.C. 344.

of openness – quite possibly symptoms of such confusion.[81] Clarifying the structure of the country's highest court may help combat this.

A problem of resources

"There's another issue that underlies this, not of policy but of pragmatism: the accommodation for the law lords in the Palace of Westminster is appalling. The amount of room available to them has a real impact on the effectiveness of their work. The example I'm aware of is Research Assistants: not every law lord has one, simply because there isn't enough space for each to have one. It's not a question of not having the money or anything like that or law lords not wanting them, there's just not the physical space to accommodate them – the law lords' rooms are actually quite tiny. All of this is inappropriate. There is an incredibly strong pragmatic case for saying this court should be located elsewhere." – **Dr Christopher Forsyth**

Several articles and many of our interviewees advocating reform of the highest court have stressed that the House of Lords simply cannot provide the resources that the law lords require in order to dispatch justice in an appropriately efficient manner. It may be the apex of the legal system, but judges, litigants, barristers and solicitors alike enjoy better facilities in the lower courts. The resources available to the Appellate Committee reflect the reality that it is institutionally nothing more than a committee of the House of Lords. The law lords' administration works in very cramped conditions; one law lord does not even have a room, and another's office is said to be a converted lavatory.[82] Lord Bingham, the Senior Law Lord, has remarked: *"I doubt if any supreme court anywhere in the developed world is as cramped as our own."*[83]

---

81   See Genn, *Paths to Justice: What People Do and Think about Going to Law* (Hart Publishing, 1999) pp.239-247.

82   Sir Sydney Kentridge, *The Highest Court: Selecting the Judges* (2003) 62 C.L.J. 55.

83   Lord Bingham, *The Evolving Constitution*, lecture to JUSTICE, October 2001.

This predicament has important adverse effects. The location is not conducive to public accessibility, despite hosting the highest court in the country – no doubt another kick in the teeth for public confidence in the judiciary. There is minimal room for essential support staff; the principal assistance provided to the law lords is from a handful of very junior barristers who are employed on a one-year fixed term basis.

> "In the Supreme Court in the States, the offices are palatial and there are around eighty research assistants who graduated summa cum laude from Harvard Law School. All that kind of stuff is miles ahead of what we have." – **Michael Beloff QC**

Even the smooth running of hearings themselves is affected, as Robin Allen QC told us from first-hand experience:

> *"It's a joke. A complete, total joke. If I'm trying to note what my opponent is saying, I've just got a small piece of table – there's nowhere even to plug in a laptop! The law lords can't pull up cases on computer screens, or do a quick search from their desks. It's totally nineteenth century."*

In 2000, the Appellate Committee's backlog of cases stood at the sizeable figure of 94, an increase from 66, 53 and 66 from the previous three years. Faced with these pressures, the last thing that the law lords need is for their administration of justice to be slowed down by insufficient resources.

The problem cannot be resolved whilst appeals are still heard within the Palace of Westminster: *"Space within the Palace…is at a premium, especially at the House of Lords end of the building."*[84] The

---

84   *Constitutional Reform: A Supreme Court for the United Kingdom* (Department for Constitutional Affairs, July 2003), p.12

position cannot be improved without asking other peers to give up their desks; this will not, and should not happen, the House's primary function being a legislature, not a court. A physical move was inevitable.

However, there are some who do not believe this argument to be decisive. Dr Christopher Forsyth summed their point:

> *"The practical case justifies a move to Somerset House or wherever – it doesn't justify necessarily breaking the link with the House of Lords. The law lords could sit in appropriate accommodation, doubtlessly in London, but that would not prevent them from remaining members of the House of Lords."*

It is certainly true that provisions could be made for the law lords to sit in a separate, fully-resourced building whilst retaining their legislative role. However, if the effort and expense of physically 'outsourcing' the law lords is indeed to be undertaken – a hugely significant change in its own right – those who advocate physical but not institutional separation must provide some rational arguments for keeping the law lords in the legislature, arguments which outweigh the other problems with the current system that we have already discussed.

Arguments Against Reform

The law lords' role in Parliamentary debates

"We shall lose more than we shall gain if the highest court is taken out of the Lords." – Rt Hon Sir Nicholas Lyell QC

The most frequent and influential argument in favour of the current system cites the benefit that the law lords gain from sitting in Parliament and the corresponding advantage that Parliament enjoys from having the law lords within its membership. The point was encapsulated in a recent article by Lord Rees-Mogg:

> *"Removing the law lords to a quiet court of their own will not benefit Parliament – they do not intervene in the House of Lords on political matters, but they do give their opinions, if only rarely, on legal and judicial matters. The House of Lords has been very good on law, much better than the Commons. This owes much to the law lords....*
> *It does not harm the law lords themselves to be embedded in Parliament; they are more conscious of the lawmaking process than judges who have no direct experience of legislation."*[85]

The first side of this argument – that the law lords grow as judges by seeing things as legislators – was made famous by Lord Wilberforce, widely regarded as one of the greatest judges of the last century. Ross Cranston QC MP expressed some sympathy with this notion:

> *"I think one of the difficulties with the way we recruit judges is that, although they're excellent in so many ways, they don't have a great range of experience. They've been to the Bar, and been outstandingly successful and they've got the brains to be judges, but some of them don't always have a range of experience. Therefore, as our highest judges are part of the legislature, they can, by osmosis, come to understand the difficulties, the limitations, the whole ranges of pressures that a government sometimes faces. Another example is that one of the law lords always chairs the European Sub-Committee*

---

85   William Rees-Mogg, *The Times*, 4th August 2003.

in the House of Lords. I think that has given the judges who've chaired the committee another insight which they would otherwise not have had, because they haven't done EC work."

However, this is not a decisive argument in favour of keeping the highest court within the legislature. There are plenty of other means through which the law lords can – and no doubt already do – easily remain abreast of current political and social issues. Indeed, sensitivity to such issues is already a key criterion in the existing scheme for appointments to judicial office, and is likely to become even more so in the future.[86] Surely lack of expertise in a particular area of law would best be remedied through training schemes and/or private study, rather than by sitting on a legislative committee covering the same subject.[87] Moreover, if this so-called 'Wilberforce Argument' were valid, it would surely be applicable to judges of the Court of Appeal and of the High Court – none of whom sit in the legislature.

There is no doubt that the House of Lords, as a body that scrutinises proposed legislation, has much to benefit from containing individuals with the legal expertise and experience of the law lords. To quote Michael Beloff QC:

"These are a group of alpha plus people, certainly compared to some of the people in that body. What they say is obviously always worth listening to. It's rather a pity to have a debate about law reform or criminal justice and so on without the input of those who really know what's going on."

---

86 See p.129ff.
87 Training schemes for judges on up-and-coming areas of law, run by academic and professional experts, already exist. For example, upon the passing of the Human Rights Act in 1998, the government set aside £5 million for training judges and magistrates in this field.

Dr Christopher Forsyth suspected that, in this respect, the government might have had somewhat Machiavellian motives in proposing to abolish the Appellate Committee:

> *"One wonders whether the Government would prefer not to have this eminent group of judges sitting in the House of Lords being able to make well-informed pungent and telling criticisms of the details of legal reform measures that come before the House. It's better for the government to have them out of the way. Not a party political point – I'm sure other governments would be of much the same sort of mind; they don't want that kind of judicial scrutiny of the nuts and bolts, particularly on these big issues such as trial by jury or whatever. They don't want that kind of high-powered judicial scrutiny and judges being prepared to talk on that basis and therefore want them out of the way."*[88]

Nonetheless, we do not find this point decisive either, for two reasons. Firstly, the extent to which serving law lords are able to participate in Parliamentary debate is increasingly limited. Pressures of time limit their availability: their overwhelming priority is judging, which, as Lord Phillips has recently emphasised, is a full time job. Article 6(1) and Lord Bingham's practice statement have also made a substantial difference.[89] The practice statement suggests that judges should refrain from expressing an opinion on a matter which might later be relevant to an appeal to the House.[90] If a judge were to break that protocol, then in light of the aforementioned case law on Article 6(1) ECHR, his Parliamentary speech may form the basis of a legal challenge to invalidate his judgment.[91] For example, law lords may no longer insist in a debate that

---

88   A sentiment shared by the former Lord Chancellor, Lord Mackay – see Clare Dyer, *Top Judges 'Face Being Gagged'*, *The Guardian*, 16th September 2003.

89   See pp32–33

90   H.L. Debs., col. 419, 22 June 2000.

91   See pp 2833.

proposed legislation is or is not incompatible with the Human Rights Act, without jeopardising the validity of their judgment in a subsequent legal case seeking a 'declaration of incompatibility' of that legislation with the Human Rights Act[92]. Consequently, judicial contributions to House of Lords debates have become almost negligible. In the two years following Lord Bingham's practice statement, only three of the twelve Lords of Appeal in Ordinary spoke in the House.[93] Law lords rightly do not want to hamper their primary function – sitting as judges – through exercising their subordinate role as legislators.

No wonder then, the Senior Law Lord's insistence in 2002 that:

"...the law lords are not legislators and do not belong in a House to whose business they can make no more than a slight contribution."[94]

Secondly, as Michael Beloff QC went on to acknowledge, the law lords' expertise, whilst exceptional, is not altogether unique. There are other legal experts of a similar calibre who may advise Parliament instead. One option, put forward in the Government's consultation paper on the Supreme Court,[95] would be the establishment of a convention whereby retired members of the Supreme Court are appointed to the House of Lords. Subject to certain considerations, discussed later, we support this proposal.[96] If it were enacted, the legislature would continue to receive the first-hand advice of some of the most respected and experienced judges in the land, who – unlike the sitting law lords – would be able to contribute as full-time legislators.

---

92 Human Rights Act 1998, s.4.
93 Lord Hope, Hutton and Scott – see *A Supreme Court for the United Kingdom* (JUSTICE Briefing Paper, May 2003) – referring to the period 22nd June 2000 to 23rd May 2002.
94 Lord Bingham. *A Supreme Court for the United Kingdom*, lecture to The Constitution Unit, May 1st 2002.
95 *Constitutional Reform: A Supreme Court for the United Kingdom* (Department for Constitutional Affairs, July 2003), p.27.
96 See pp. 72–74

Even if it did not contain retired judges, the House of Lords – whether fully elected or retaining an appointed element – would in all probability always contain leading lawyers who, whilst never having held judicial office, are of a comparable legal calibre and would more than meet the task of scrutinising relevant legislative proposals. Already, the bulk of legal expertise communicated to the House in debates on legislation comes from leading QCs who are regarded as being at the top of their profession (such as Lords Lester and Alexander), rather than from the law lords. In the unlikely event that a future fully-elected House of Lords were really to suffer from a deficiency of legal expertise, it could set up a committee to hear the views of former judges and leading practitioners – or even grant them *ad hoc* speaking rights in the Chamber.

Waiting for the dust of constitutional reform to settle

One of the arguments put forward by Lord Irvine against reform or abolition of the House of Lords Appellate Committee was that the other constitutional reforms should be allowed to 'bed down' before changes to the top level courts are contemplated.[97] However, Le Sueur and Cornes offer a convincing rebuttal of this argument:

> *"Waiting for a time free of future uncertainty about the context in which the UK's top courts will operate is like waiting for Godot: it will never arrive...* [Besides,] *the bedding down argument wrongly views the UK's top courts as passive reactors to change rather than being part of the process of change."* [98]

As we noted earlier, the law lords' position ought to have been consid-

---

97   H.L. Debs., col. 1983, 28 October 1998.
98   Le Sueur & Cornes, *The Future of the United Kingdom's Highest Courts* (The Constitution Unit, 2001), p.52.

ered *in the context of* the Labour Government's prior constitutional reform.[99] This is demonstrated by the fact that, if just eighteen more MPs had voted in favour of an all-elected House of Lords on 4th February 2003, the law lords would have been removed from the House without any consideration of the legal and constitutional arguments regarding their own particular future.

No longer a peerage – a stint on ambition?

This point was put to us by Dr Christopher Forsyth:

"It seems that the judges of the new court will not be peers of the realm. But that actually changes the career path and possibly the career decisions of the really ambitious barrister. For every hundred who start thinking 'I'm going to become a law lord', perhaps one or less than one of them actually does; but, that bright barrister who starts off in this way has a certain path in mind that culminates with one of the very highest honours that our society can give to successful individuals, namely a peerage. Now it's going to be different; you'll culminate in being a JSC ['Judge of the Supreme Court'] or whatever it may be – I think that's a significant difference; it's going to change the career path of ambitious and able individuals."

It is possible that the discontinuance of peerages for judges of the highest court may act as a disincentive for the highly ambitious and talented. However, the extent to which this will have an effect is not such as to make the argument decisive. Moreover, some mitigation against this problem might be provided in our recommendation that Supreme Court judges keep the title 'Lord of Appeal' even though they will not be peers of the realm.[100]

---

99   See pp. 19–20
100   See p.72

The benefits of tradition

Whilst the House of Lords' judicial role has ancient origins, the system as we now know it is hardly old enough to be classed as a political or cultural 'tradition'. Only a little over one hundred years ago, 'lay' peers were able to participate in the House's judicial work, and the Appellate Committee itself dates back only to 1948, when post-War building work forced the law lords out of the Chamber in the Palace of Westminster. So as Le Sueurand Comes observe:[101]

> "Those of a conservative turn of mind cannot...simply call in aid tradition or invoke venerable ages of institutions as the basis for preserving the current arrangements at the apex of the UK's court system"

Summary: Why Reform Was Necessary

None of the points put forward in favour of keeping judges of the highest court within the legislature are of any significant weight. In fact, this is unsurprising, since the reasons why the House of Lords has come to act as a final appeal court are historical rather than doctrinal.[102] On the other hand, the case for change is supported by a number of cogent arguments. Resource limitations facing the Appellate Committee have reached breaking point – a physical move out of the Palace of Westminster is necessary if justice is to be administered efficiently. Coupled with this is the inevitability of a challenge to the present system under Article 6 ECHR, and a growing realisation that the objections in principle to judges sitting as legislators have adverse practical effects on the public perception of the justice system. Recent

---

101   Le Sueur & Cornes, *The Future of the United Kingdom's Highest Courts* (The Constitution Unit, 2001), p.71.

102   See p.22.

MORI polls show that public confidence in the judiciary now stands at a mere 59.5% - twenty per cent less than in the United States. The public rate judges even lower than accountants, the traditional butt of many a popular jibe.[103] Clarifying the constitutional position of the United Kingdom's highest court – making clear that it is an independent guardian of the rule of law, with its judges having no perceived commitment to one side of certain cases as a result of their part-time legislative role – will go some way to addressing this problem. Therefore, whilst the Government deserves heavy criticism for the way in which its proposals for a new Supreme Court were announced, the core substance of those proposals is to be welcomed.

---

103 Average of four MORI polls, January 1999 – February 2002. The net satisfaction/dissatisfaction figure for judges was 45.25%; for accountants it was 49.75%. By way of comparison, doctors scored 85.25%, teachers 78% and the police 50.25%.

2. The New Supreme Court – Its Functions and Powers

What Kind of Court?

We now turn to the question of what model the Appellate Committee's replacement should take. At the outset, it should be noted that, although at various points there have been calls – in particular from the Labour benches – for the third tier of appeal to be abolished altogether, there is currently an overwhelming consensus that an appeal court above the Court of Appeal of England and Wales and the Court of Appeal in Northern Ireland is desirable.[1] We agree.

Three kinds of court have been seriously discussed by proponents of reform: a supra-legislative supreme court that can strike down legislation; a constitutional court; or a final appeal court with the same structure and powers as the Appellate Committee. In spite of the Government's insistence that it is undergoing extensive consultation on its plans for a new court, the Department for Constitutional

---

1   Le Sueur and Cornes, *Future of the United Kingdom's Highest Courts* (The Constitution Unit, 2001), p.10.

Affairs' consultation paper automatically assumes that the third of these models will be adopted and does not ask for suggestions as to the alternatives.[2]

At present, the first of these alternatives would, in all probability, be constitutionally impossible. The establishment of a supra-legislative court which may strike down 'unconstitutional' legislation necessarily requires the creation of a framework of entrenched rights (such as a written constitution) that takes precedence over 'ordinary' Acts of Parliament. According to the orthodox doctrine of Parliamentary sovereignty, it is impossible for Parliament to entrench such a framework.[3] To break out of this deadlock would require a monumental constitutional shift that the current reforms do not provide;[4] how that might be done and whether it is desirable are questions outside our remit.

In the second model, a specialist court would sit as the apex for appeals in 'constitutional cases'. Le Sueur and Cornes suggest that such a court's jurisdiction might include: 'devolution issues';[5] cases where the question at issue was whether to grant a *"declaration of incompatibility"* of an Act of Parliament with Convention rights;[6] cases turning on Section 6(1) of the Human Rights Act 1998;[7] judicial review, habeas corpus and other statutory applications commenced in the Administrative Court and analogous procedures in Scotland and Northern Ireland; appeals arising from the proposed Northern Ireland Bill of Rights.[8] A necessary corollary would be another top

---

2   *Constitutional Reform: A Supreme Court for the United Kingdom* (Department for Constitutional Affairs, July 2003), pp.20-23.
3   See Bradley and Ewing, *Constitutional and Administrative Law* (Longman, 13th edn, 2003), ch.4; Loveland, *Constitutional Law* (Butterworths, 2nd edn., 2000), ch.2.
4   See Wade, *The Basis of Legal Sovereignty* (1955) C.L.J. 172.
5   Arising out of the Scotland Act, Northern Ireland Act and Government of Wales Act 1998 – See pp. 59 ff.
6   Human Rights Act 1998, s.4
7   *"It is unlawful for a public authority to act in a way which is incompatible with a Convention right."*
8   Le Sueur and Cornes, *Future of the United Kingdom's Highest Courts* (The Constitution Unit, 2001), pp 87-88.

level court for dealing with 'non-constitutional' matters. The two courts could be entirely distinct, or sit as separate 'divisions' within an over-arching court of final instance with the same secretariat and premises.[9]

It is surprising that the Government has not seen fit even to consult on this possibility in its 'consultation paper', since there have, in recent years, been a number of calls for some kind of UK constitutional court. These have included: the Scottish National Party;[10] Lord Steel of Aikwood;[11] Lord Cooke of Thorndon (the former President of the New Zealand Court of Appeal who has sat on the Appellate Committee);[12] Lord Lester of Herne Hill QC;[13] Richard Gordon QC;[14] Aiden O'Neill QC.[15] Even Lord Wilberforce gave *"general support"* to the idea in 1998.[16] Advocates of a constitutional court emphasise the benefits of speciality and expertise in an area of law that is particularly idiosyncratic and increasingly important:

> *"The reasons pertain to experience, expertise, specialisation, and temperament. Lord X may be admirably equipped to decide issues of domestic law, but by experience, interest and temperament may not be so well qualified to deal with human rights questions.... It tends to be a field of its own and there is much to be said for a court of its own.... It would be a somewhat specialised, dedicated court, a limited corps of specialised judges."[17]*

---

9   *ibid.*
10   H.C. Debs., col. 204, 12 May 1998.
11   H.L. Debs., col. 1963, 28 October 1998.
12   H.L. Debs., col. 1967, 28 October 1998.
13   However, Lord Lester told us in his interview that he is now more ambivalent as to the desirability of this model.
14   Gordon and Wilmot-Smith (eds.) *Human Rights in the United Kingdom* (Oxford University Press, 1996).
15   O'Neill, *Judicial Politics in the Judicial Committee, Journal of the Law Society of Scotland*, 1 January 2001.
16   H.L. Debs., col. 1966, 28 October 1998.

"A specialist court could also adapt its procedures and approaches better to deal with public law litigation. Third party interventions and the use of amici curiae are likely to be more frequent in this field than others."[18]

"It would prevent [a single highest court] *having the character of its caseload swamped with public law cases at the expense of commercial law, tort law and other fields in which it currently adjudicates. It will also prevent delays...caused by the need for devolution issues ... to have priority over the ordinary work of the House of Lords."*[19]

However, there are a number of problems with a constitutional court, which proponents of the model have so far been unable to surmount. Most importantly, such a model would run counter to the traditional British position, compounded by the scheme of the Human Rights Act 1998, that *"constitutional issues are not a separate category of legal problem, but suffuse all aspects of the law and are to be adjudicated on by the ordinary courts."*[20] In the absence of a codified constitution, it would be difficult – even under Le Sueur and Cornes' specified model – to distinguish clearly between 'constitutional' and 'non-constitutional' cases. The extensive case law on the public-private law divide demonstrates the real danger that large amounts of time and money will be spent in litigation on this potentially irresolvable issue of demarcation.[21]

---

17   Lord Cook of Thorndon, H.L. Debs., col. 1967, 28 October 1998.
18   Le Sueur and Cornes, *Future of the United Kingdom's Highest Courts* (The Constitution Unit, 2001), p.89.
19   *ibid.*
20   *A Supreme Court for the United Kingdom* (JUSTICE Briefing Paper, May 2003).
21   See Lord Bingham, *The Evolving Constitution*, lecture to JUSTICE, October 2001; *A Supreme Court for the United Kingdom* (JUSTICE Briefing Paper, May 2003); Le Sueur and Cornes, *Future of the United Kingdom's Highest Courts* (The Constitution Unit, 2001), p.90.

"You'd spend an enormous amount of time and resources on the added question, what is a constitutional issue? You'd have jurisdictional questions which would enormously entertaining and profitable for the lawyers. But as it is, the common law constitution which we have, which is of course not unwritten but merely uncodified, doesn't make a distinction between what is a proposition of the constitution and what is an ordinary proposition of law. Although I have various views about constitutional rights and statutes, I don't think we should go down the route of inventing a court that would require rigid distinctions to be made that don't need to be made for the proper operation of our legal system and would potentially be very wasteful of time and resources." – **Lord Justice Laws**

An additional worry is the likelihood that the specialist workload of a constitutional court would soon render it a *political* institution, thereby compromising the fundamental concept of judicial independence on which proposals for reform are largely based[22]. There is also a possibility of tension between the constitutional and 'non-constitutional' final courts as they compete for prestige, a problem avoided as between the Appellate Committee of the House of Lords and the Judicial Committee of the Privy Council since they are largely composed of the same judges.[23]

Therefore, whilst the question is a live one and should have been included in the Government's consultation process, on balance we conclude that the constitutional court model is undesirable. Rather, a final appeal court with the same powers and structure as the existing Appellate Committee appears preferable.[24] However, we take issue with the Government's approach to the naming of this

---

22 See Le Sueur and Cornes, *Future of the United Kingdom's Highest Courts* (The Constitution Unit, 2001), p.91.

23 *ibid.*

24 A fourth model, based on the operated by the European Court of Justice, where questions as to the meaning of the law are referred for definitive ruling, is swiftly – and rightly – dismissed by all the leading proponents of reform as inapplicable to our legal system. The EU situation is very different, requiring as it does a common meaning of EU Law across all the Member States.

25 And as Lord Bingham has also highlighted – *The Evolving Constitution*, lecture to JUSTICE, October 2001.

court. As Dr Christopher Forsyth and Professor Ian Loveland emphasised to us,[25] for many people, the mention of a single body called the 'Supreme Court' conjures up the image of the Supreme Court of the United States of America, striking down legislation and asserting the primacy of an entrenched constitution. We agree with Dr Forsyth that:

> "We don't want to encourage confusion or borrow inappropriately the aura of the US Court, so if we're going to have this new court a better name would be the one used in Hong Kong and other places: the Court of Final Appeal."[26]

The replacement of the Appellate Committee with a court which is institutionally independent from the legislature is motivated in part by the argument that such a move would clarify the constitutional position of the highest court in the land and increase public understanding of the justice system. To then go and give the new court a name with false connotations would limit those advantages.

Moreover, there already exists a Supreme Court of Judicature in England and Wales. This is not one court, but the collective name given to the Crown Court, the Court of Appeal and the High Court.[27] The Department for Constitutional Affairs' consultation paper automatically assumes that this collective name will change, in order for the highest court to be called the 'Supreme Court'. It asks simply: *"what should the existing Supreme Court be renamed?"*[28] The more pertinent

---

26   We will, however, continue to refer to the court by its proposed name of 'Supreme Court', in order to avoid confusion.

27   Since the component courts have their own names (eg. 'Court of Appeal'), by which they are commonly known, the title 'Supreme Court' is perhaps less confusing here than it would be if it were applied to the highest court alone as its sole name.

28   *Constitutional Reform: A Supreme Court for the United Kingdom* (Department for Constitutional Affairs, July 2003), p.40.

question – whether it is appropriate for the new court to take that name at all – has been entirely passed over.

Jurisdiction

'Devolution issues' and Scottish criminal law

Under the Scotland Act 1998, the Government of Wales Act 1998 and the Northern Ireland Act 1998, the Judicial Committee of the Privy Council is the final court of appeal for legal cases in which it is claimed that the devolved institutions have acted outside their powers. The first question in the Department for Constitutional Affairs' consultation paper on the Supreme Court asks whether the new court's jurisdiction should take over such 'devolution issues' from the Judicial Committee.[29] The Government has made clear that it favours such a move.[30]

The principal argument for the Supreme Court to assume the Privy Council's jurisdiction over devolution issues is that it would restore *"a single apex to the UK's judicial systems."*[31] Until 1998, the Appellate Committee was bound by no other court, and judgments of the Judicial Committee were merely persuasive. Now, the Judicial Committee's decisions in cases heard under the devolution Acts are binding *"in all legal proceedings"*[32] – in other words, they take precedence even over rulings from the Appellate Committee.[33] Because such cases may involve alleged breaches of ECHR rights by the devolved institutions,[34] this means that the Judicial Committee has the final domestic word on

---

29 *Constitutional Reform: A Supreme Court for the United Kingdom* (Department for Constitutional Affairs, July 2003), p.20
30 *Ibid.*
31 *Ibid.*
32 Scotland Act 1998, s. 103(1); Northern Ireland Act 1998, s.82(1); Government of Wales Act 1998, Schedule 8, paragraph 32(b).
33 This is abundantly clear by reference to the *Hansard* record of debates on the Scotland Bill – e.g. Lord Sewel H.L. Debs., col. 619, 8 October 1998].
34 Breach of Convention right by a devolved institution being outside its powers under the devolution legislation.

the interpretation of the Convention. In principle, it seems wrong for the Supreme Court of the United Kingdom to be bound by the Privy Council, with its much lower profile and otherwise diminishing jurisdiction, on such a fundamental area as human rights – which permeates not only administrative law but right through employment law, planning law, media law and many other fields.

A real potential for a clash between twin apexes was demonstrated – and nearly realised – in the course of two recent cases, which alleged that town and country planning procedures breached Article 6(1) ECHR. The Scottish case was decided in July 2000 by the Outer House ruling that there was a breach.[35] The English case was heard by the High Court in December 2000, with the same conclusion,[36] but went to appeal, which was heard very swiftly by the House of Lords Appellate Committee in May 2001. What if the Scottish case had gone to appeal before the Judicial Committee of the Privy Council beforehand, and reached a different outcome before the judgment in the English case was delivered?[37] The Appellate Committee would have had to make an about-turn and toe the Judicial Committee's line. Such a conflict between the top level courts is, in our view, undesirable.

The reasons for giving the devolution jusrisdiction issues to the Judicial Committee in the first place are not entirely clear. During the passage of the Scotland Bill, Lord Wilberforce pointed out that the Government had offered *"no reasoned explanation"* for the move.[38] As Michael Beloff QC pointed out, the most likely motive was that the Appellate Committee's existence as part of House of Lords rendered it an inappropriate stage to hear division of powers disputes between the

---

35   *County Properties Ltd v Scottish Ministers* [2000] S.L.T. 965.
36   *R (Holding and Barnes plc) v Secretary of State for the Environment, Transport and the Regions* ['the Alconbury case'] [2001] Administrative Court Digest 65.
37   For a full account of this saga, see Le Sueur and Cornes, *The Future of the United Kingdom's Highest Courts* (The Constitution Unit, 2001), pp.79-80.
38   H.L. Debs., col. 1966 28 October 1998.

Westminster Parliament and Belfast, Cardiff or Edinburgh.[39] This was cited in the Department for Constitutional Affairs' consultation paper on the Supreme Court as the key reason behind the move.[40] The paper also correctly observes that, once the highest court is removed from the legislature, this problem disappears. Therefore, the Government concludes, devolution jurisdiction should be assumed by the Supreme Court in order to eliminate the hierarchical problems outlined above.

We agree with this proposal. The other arguments in favour of the Judicial Committee having jurisdiction over devolution issues are either weak or surmountable. The Judicial Committee's *"experience of handling cases that raise constitutional issues"*[41] makes little difference, since the Judicial Committee is usually constituted in large part from among the law lords themselves. For the same reason, the argument that the Appellate Committee's workload would be overburdened if it were to be given jurisdiction over devolution issues is specious. Whilst there are a greater number of Scottish and Irish judges able to sit on the Judicial Committee than on the Appellate Committee, this cannot be decisive; further judges from Scotland and Northern Ireland can always be appointed to the Supreme Court if its devolution jurisdiction so required.[42]

The Scotland Act 1998 allows, for the first time, a court in London to hear Scottish criminal appeals – albeit only where the appeal is based upon the alleged breach of a Convention right by one of the devolved institutions.[43] In 2001, an academic report expressed sympathy with

---

39   See also Le Sueur and Cornes, *The Future of the United Kingdom's Highest Courts* (The Constitution Unit, 2001), p.79.
40   *Constitutional Reform: A Supreme Court for the United Kingdom* (Department for Constitutional Affairs, July 2003), p.19.
41   Cited as a reason for giving it jurisdiction over devolution issues by the junior minister Win Griffiths MP during the passage of the devolution legislation through the House of Commons of the devolution legislation [HC Debs 3 Feb 1998, col. 927].
42   See pp. 68–69
43   If a Convention right is breached by a Scottish criminal court then appeal lies only to Scotland's final court of appeal in criminal matters, the High Court of Justiciary.

arguments for a further step: that a new Supreme Court should have jurisdiction to hear *all* criminal appeals from Scotland, whether or not they raise devolution issues[44]. However, this idea has been rejected by the Government in the aftermath of its recent proposals for judicial reform,[45] and rightly so. There are huge differences between English and Scottish criminal law, which Lord Hope, one of the current law lords, has described as resembling the differences between *"two foreign countries."*[46] The new Supreme Court, containing a majority of non-Scottish members, would, therefore, be an inherently inappropriate final appeal court for Scottish criminal cases. We disagree with the counter-argument that law lords have always had to acquire a detailed knowledge of the areas of law in which they had no previous expertise;[47] there is a clear difference between learning a new area of the same country's law and learning the law of a new country altogether, the latter effectively being the case with regard to an English lawyer learning Scottish criminal law.

The remaining Privy Council jurisdiction

The Judicial Committee of the Privy Council would accordingly be left with appeals from a number of Commonwealth countries and overseas territories, as well as a small ecclesiastical jurisdiction.[48] Its jurisdiction is set to shrink even further. New Zealand, from where eighteen per

---

44   Le Sueur and Cornes, *The Future of the United Kingdom's Highest Courts* (The Constitution Unit, 2001), p.70.

45   *Constitutional Reform: A Supreme Court for the United Kingdom* (Department for Constitutional Affairs, July 2003), p.22.

46   *R v Manchester Stipendiary Magistrate ex parte Granada Television Ltd* [2000] 2 WLR 1 at p.5. Lord Bingham, the Senior Law Lord, took the same position in his lecture *The Evolving Constitution* in October 2001.

47   Le Sueur and Cornes, *The Future of the United Kingdom's Highest Courts* (The Constitution Unit, 2001), p.70.

48   Specifically, against Church of England Pastoral Measures. Jurisdiction over appeals against decisions of governing bodies in certain healthcare professions has recently been transferred from the Privy Council to the High Court and Court of Session, under the NHS Reform and Health Care Professions Act 2002.

cent of the Judicial Committee's case load came in 1999, is set to pass legislation by the end of 2003 that will sever its ties.[49] The proposed Caribbean Court of Justice appears set, once it is finally established, to replace the Judicial Committee as the final court of appeal for several Caribbean states; from November 1996 to November 1999, cases from those states represented forty-six per cent of the Judicial Committee's work.[50] At this rate, *"it is likely that in the medium term the Judicial Committee will receive little more than a dozen appeals a year from the overseas legal systems."*[51] Ross Cranston's suggestion to us that within the foreseeable future the caseload would completely *"dry up"* is, for better or worse, highly plausible.

Consequently, there have been calls for the new Supreme Court to swallow up the Judicial Committee's 'rump' jurisdiction upon its creation.[52] Against this, it is said that supreme Court would most likely be unappealing to the countries concerned, since, unlike the Judicial Committee in its Commonwealth jurisdiction, it would be viewed as a domestic court of the United Kingdom.[53] To some commentators, that does not matter:

> *"Tough. If our Supreme Court is not good enough for them, they can take their appeals elsewhere. If they value our expertise, however, they are unlikely to mind if it is delivered in a different court."*[54]

However, all the interviewees whom we questioned on this point

---

49   The New Zealand Government's proposal has met with strong opposition, but the Green Party's support is set swing the vote in its favour. See Helen Tunnah, *New Final Appeal Court by Next Year*, New Zealand Herald, 17th September 2003

50   See Le Sueur and Cornes, *The Future of the United Kingdom's Highest Courts* (The Constitution Unit, 2001), p. 103.

51   *ibid*, p.105.

52   For example, Joshua Rozenberg, *The Daily Telegraph*, 26th June 2003.

53   See *A Supreme Court for the United Kingdom* (JUSTICE Briefing Paper, May 2003); Lord Bingham, *The Evolving Constitution*, lecture to JUSTICE, October 2001.

54   Joshua Rozenberg, *The Daily Telegraph*, 26th June 2003.

thought that any transfer of the Commonwealth jurisdiction to the Supreme Court should not come as part of the immediate domestic judicial reform programme, but rather is a matter for the individual states themselves to decide. We agree: to impose a new system upon these independent nations and then to say "lump it or leave it" would run against the spirit of the Commonwealth.[55]

There does appear to be wide support, on the basis of practical efficiency, for the Judicial Committee to be housed within the Supreme Court building, with an effectively unified administration.[56] Whilst not merging them into one formal court, this would provide the Judicial Committee with the same state of the art on-site resources that the Supreme Court appears set to enjoy, would save having to ferry Supreme Court judges over to Downing Street and back (their time being a valuable commodity), and would promote transparency.[57] Such an arrangement would also undoubtedly be less expensive. The Government is wrong to dismiss it without consultation. The Department for Constitutional Affairs' consultation paper on the Supreme Court simply insists that *"the administrative and support arrangements for the Judicial Committee would...remain unchanged"* because the right of senior judges who are Privy Counsellors but not law lords to sit in the Judicial Committee will not change under the new system.[58] How this supports keeping the Judicial Committee where

---

55   We agree with Le Sueur and Cornes, *The Future of the United Kingdom's Highest Courts* (The Constitution Unit, 2001), p. 108, that the (albeit rare) appeals heard by the Judicial Committee under Church of England Pastoral Measures, which deal, in essence, with the reorganization of the parishes, might more appropriately be dealt with at High Court level by the Administrative Court – as are disputes about many other Church of England matters.

56   *A Supreme Court for the United Kingdom* (JUSTICE Briefing Paper, May 2003); Lord Bingham, *The Evolving Constitution*, lecture to JUSTICE, October 2001; Le Sueur and Cornes *The Future of the United Kingdom's Highest Courts* (The Constitution Unit, 2001), p.105.

57   The Judicial Committee's work is currently obscure to the untrained eye; it sits in Downing Street, shut off from the open world, and, whilst hearings are technically public, no details on public access are provided on the Privy Council's website.

58   *Constitutional Reform: A Supreme Court for the United Kingdom* (Department for Constitutional Affairs, July 2003), p.23.

it is or counters any of the above arguments in favour of moving it is not stated, and remains unclear. Certainly, the new Supreme Court building, wherever it may be, will be able to cope with the occasional influx of a few extra judges to sit alongside members of the Supreme Court on Commonwealth appeals.

Personnel

We shall evaluate the Government's proposals for appointments to the judiciary and examine various alternative models in Chapter Four. This section concentrates on issues such as the number, composition, title and tenure of those appointed.

Full-time members

In a recent influential article advocating a Supreme Court, Lord Steyn expressed hope that it *"would not be larger than the existing figure of 12 law lords"* but did not elucidate upon his reasons for this desire.[59] Whilst purporting to be open to consultation on the matter, the Government agrees with his proposal.[60] Again, it is not clear why. The only argument its consultation paper offers in favour of it is that *"the larger the number of members of the court, the greater the scope for potential problems over the selection of which judges are to sit on which cases"*[61] – that is, the possibility that the composition of any particular panel of the court would affect the outcome of the case it hears – but later in the same document it concludes that the scope for such problems is minimal.[62]

The Appellate Committee usually sits in a panel of five members,

---

59 Lord Steyn, *The Case for a Supreme Court*, (2002) 118 L.Q.R. 382 at p.395

60 *Constitutional Reform: A Supreme Court for the United Kingdom* (Department for Constitutional Affairs, July 2003), p.24.

61 *ibid.*

62 *Ibid*, p.37.

which is accepted as a satisfactory arrangement.[63] A membership of twelve enables two cases to be heard simultaneously, with leeway in case one or two members are preoccupied by other duties, such as writing judgments or chairing a public inquiry. Nevertheless, there are not always enough members available for simultaneous hearings to take place and, even when there are, this has not prevented an increasing backlog of cases awaiting hearing before the Appellate Committee, which in 2000 stood at the sizeable figure of 94.[64] The proposed transfer of devolution cases to the Supreme Court may serve to increase this burden. Therefore, there would appear to be at least a prima facie case in favour of increasing the membership of the Court by between two and six.

A possible reason why the Government has not made such a proposal is that some law lords fear that an increase in their number will bring with it a decrease in their prestige. However, the Court of Appeal has a maximum of thirty-seven ordinary members and manages to command great authority and respect. By sheer propor-tion, fifteen or seventeen out of over one thousand full-time judges in the country is as much of an elite as twelve out of the same number.[65] The outstanding calibre of senior judges outside the Appellate Committee demonstrates that the presence of a few extra members will in no way dilute the intellectual quality of the Supreme Court. In fact, a possible consequence of such a move would be to broaden the expertise of the court, since some of the extra members

---

63   None of the interviewees we asked considered that the idea of the Supreme Court sitting *en banc* was either realistic (in terms of combating the caseload before it) or an improvement (in terms of pooling expertise and/or avoiding cases being determined by the identity of the judges on the panel).

64   See p.42.

65   The total number of Lord Justices of Appeal, High Court Judges, Circuit Judges and District Judges in 2000-2001 was 1112 [Court Service Plan, 2000-2003].

66   Le Sueur and Cornes, *Future of the United Kingdom's Highest Courts* (The Constitution Unit, 2001), p.70, note that in 2001, *"none of the current law lords were, for instance, specialists in English family law or UK immigration law before appointment."*

might well have a prior background in a different area of law from those previously practised by the existing twelve,[66] The availability of former law lords to sit on the Appellate Committee when they are needed to 'make up the numbers' does not detract from the arguments in favour of increasing the permanent membership; it is not fitting for the efficiency of the highest court in the country to depend upon the retired.

Against all this, Lord Lester of Herne Hill QC insisted to us that the Appellate Committee's backlog depends not so much upon a lack of law lords as upon the pitiful resources available to them in the Palace of Westminster.[67] Richard Cornes has recently noted that *"comparable common law supreme courts, even those which deal with some of their cases in panels, have fewer judges"* than the Appellate Committee and yet manage to operate efficiently.[68]

Ultimately, it is impossible to foretell how the creation of a fully-resourced Supreme Court will affect the case backlog, and so we suggest that no change in terms of membership numbers should be made at this stage; however, the possibility should certainly not be ruled out in the mid-term.

The reserve list

Since the removal of highest court from Parliament is substantially predicated upon the ground that it is undesirable for judges to sit as legislators, it is also necessary to abolish the present rule that the Appellate Committee may be sat upon, not only by the full-time

---

67   See pp. 41–43
68   Cornes, *The Supreme Court of the United Kingdom*, (2003) 153 New Law Journal 1018. For instance, Canada has nine, Australia has seven, and the proposed Supreme Court for New Zealand will have just five.
69   Appellate Jurisdiction Act 1876, s.5. 'High judicial office' includes the Appellate Committee, High Court, Court of Appeal and Court of Session, as well as the High Court and Court of Appeal of Northern Ireland.

Lords of Appeal in Ordinary, but also by any other member of the House of Lords who has held 'high judicial office'.[69] The most important effect of that rule has been that retired law lords may be called in to 'make up the numbers', either when some of the law lords are busy with extreme work pressures, or to provide a particular expertise on a specific case. The question remains as to whether an alternative 'reserve list' ought to be adopted for the new Supreme Court.

> "Either they are serving judges or they're not serving judges: they need to be there on a fixed panel" – **Lord Lester of Herne Hill QC**

Lord Lester and another of our consultees, Roger Smith, were emphatically opposed to part-time, retired judges sitting in the highest court. On balance, we support their arguments, which are based upon transparency and efficiency. As Mr Smith recounted:

> *"I once had a really hard time in the Court of Appeal where a judge was brought out of retirement, didn't understand what was going on, took months to decide and came out with the wrong answer. Judges need to be appointed through the commission process - you shouldn't get there by virtue of what you were. A Supreme Court can't have random odds and sods turning up to make up the numbers."*

The Government favours a reserve list, expressing concern that, if devolution cases are to be transferred from the Judicial Committee of the Privy Council – with its wider membership – to the Supreme Court, it ought to be possible to ensure that judges from the devolved nations sit on these cases. However, a convention already exists that two of the twelve law lords are from Scotland and one from Northern

Ireland.[70] These have already been shown to be sufficient in most cases.[71] If a sudden deluge of devolution cases were in future to prove otherwise, additional full-time members of the Supreme Court could always be appointed from the relevant jurisdictions.

The argument that a reserve list provides an important backup in times of extreme pressures on the law lords may also carry less weight once the Supreme Court is created, since the improved facilities and greater numbers of support staff available to the judges should substantially ease those pressures. Moreover, if New Zealand and the Caribbean countries do opt out of the Judicial Committee's jurisdiction in the near future, Supreme Court members will have about half as many Privy Council cases to hear as previously was the case.[72] If the pressures on Supreme Court judges remains so high that twelve full-time members are not enough to carry out its work, surely that is an argument for increasing the number of full-time members, rather than calling back retired judges who are nearing their eighties to sit on a part-time basis?

Moreover, the Government's suggestion that a reserve list should consist of those who have held high judicial office and are members of the Privy Council (as opposed to members of the House of Lords) has a substantial flaw.[73] In practice, only a very few senior judges other than past and present Lords of Appeal in Ordinary have also been peers, and they have usually held offices of particular eminence.[74] By contrast, it is

---

70 Although, as Cornes observes [*The Supreme Court of the United Kingdom*, (2003) 153 New Law Journal 1018], the time may soon come when the addition of a law lord with particular knowledge of the Welsh devolved institutions and language might become desirable (even though Wales and England belong to the same legal system).

71 See Cornes, *Constitutional Reform: A Supreme Court for the United Kingdom* (forthcoming article).

72 See pp. 62–64

73 *Constitutional Reform: A Supreme Court for the United Kingdom* (Department for Constitutional Affairs, July 2003), p.24. The Government would include former Supreme Court members on the reserve list for the first five years of their retirement.

74 In particular, the Lord Chief Justice, the Master of the Rolls and the President of the Court of Session in Scotland. For a definition of 'high judicial office' See p.22, n.14.

customary for all thirty-seven Court of Appeal judges to be Privy Counsellors; the Government's proposal would make all of them eligible to sit in the Supreme Court, thereby blurring the distinction between the top two courts.

Academics as members of the Supreme Court

The present qualification for appointment as a law lord is either two years' holding of high judicial office or fifteen years' standing as a barrister, advocate or solicitor in England and Wales or Scotland, or as a barrister or solicitor in Northern Ireland. Needless to say, this precludes many academics from membership.[75] Although the Government has indicated that it does not intend to change these arrangements, it has nonetheless asked for views on whether specific criteria *"for those who are not active in the courts"* should be drawn up so as to render them eligible for judicial office.[76]

Opposition to the appointment of academic lawyers to the Bench has centred on the contention that:

> "[Their] *tempo of life is quite different. It is one thing for ideas and theories to evolve and be tested over the years in the study and the lecture-room, and another thing to judge competing theories in the hot-house of the court room."*[77]

This distinction may be a good reason to preclude academics from the High Court and lower courts, but it would not apply at Supreme Court (or, indeed, Court of Appeal) level, where *"all messy issues of fact have already been resolved and the questions of law carefully defined and*

---

75 Although academics who were once called to the Bar are eligible under the fifteen-year qualification.

76 *Constitutional Reform: A Supreme Court for the United Kingdom* (Department for Constitutional Affairs, July 2003), p.36.

77 R. E. Megarry, *Lawyer and Litigant in England* (Stevens & Sons, 1962), n.27 at pp.120-122.

refined in advance of the hearing."[78] Given their wealth of expertise, it would therefore seem a potential waste to pass over very distinguished academics for consideration as members of the Supreme Court simply because they have not been in legal practice. As Lord Williams of Mostyn said in 1996:

> *"It is reasonable to suggest that if, say, Professor Glanville Williams had been in the Court of Appeal Criminal Division or in the House of Lords dealing with criminal appeals, many errors and oddities might have been avoided."*[79]

Accordingly, we support the introduction of new criteria that will make them eligible. The key criterion should be the length of the candidate's career as a professional academic in English law;[80] a requirement of fifteen years' experience would tie in with the qualification for barristers and solicitors. There should be no formal need to hold a certain academic office, since – for whatever reasons – many of the most authoritative legal scholars are not Professors or Readers.

Whilst we favour the eligibility of academics for full-time membership of the Supreme Court, we are more sceptical of the merits of their sitting on a part-time reserve list, whereby they would be called upon to sit only on specific cases where their expertise would prove especially useful. Such an approach could lead to a two-tier Supreme Court. If academics were to be part-time members only, they would inevitably only sit on particularly 'hard cases'. This could give the impression that they were in some way superior to full-time members, who would sit on all cases, and may possibly create friction between the two categories of members.

---

78 Pannick, *Judges* (Oxford University Press, 1988), p.56. The same point was made by Lord Justice Laws in his interview with us.
79 Lord Williams of Mostyn, *Judges*, in Bean (ed), *Law Reform For All* (Blackstones, 1996), p.76.
80 Or, in the case of the Supreme Court members from Scotland and Northern Ireland, in the law of those jurisdictions.

Title and tenure

Although members of the Supreme Court will not receive peerages, it seems best that – like the present law lords – they should be called 'Lords of Appeal' and accordingly bear the title 'Lord' before their name.[81] The principal alternative, *"to put the letters JSC 'Justice of the Supreme Court' after their names and give them no title beforehand,"*[82] would sit uneasily with (and possibly appear inferior to) the nomenclature of Court of Appeal judges, who are called Lord Justices of Appeal and bear the title 'Lord Justice' before their name. It would also remove one ingredient of the law lords' gravitas and authority, something which will be no less important in the Supreme Court. Continuing to call the highest judges 'Lords of Appeal' would also mitigate against Dr Christopher Forsyth's suggestion to us that the discontinuance of peerages for them may act as a disincentive for the highly ambitious and talented.[83]

The objection that this would confuse the public into thinking that the judges of the highest court were still members of the House of Lords is misguided. The high profile of the imminent extraction of these judges from the legislature and their future absence from all legislative proceedings would ensure against this. Indeed, judges of the Scottish High Court of Justiciary are called Lords and yet there is no evidence of a public perception of them as members of the House of Lords.

The Government has proposed that, whilst future members of the Supreme Court will not receive peerages, the present law lords will not lose theirs, but will simply be barred from speaking and voting whilst

---

81 As suggested by, amongst others, Professor Ian Loveland in his interview with us.
82 Suggested as one option by the Government: *Constitutional Reform: A Supreme Court for the United Kingdom* (Department for Constitutional Affairs, July 2003), p.40.
83 See p.49.
84 *Constitutional Reform: A Supreme Court for the United Kingdom* (Department for Constitutional Affairs, July 2003), p.27.

they remain judges. When they eventually retire, *"they will be free to return to the House."*[84] The Department for Constitutional Affairs' consultation paper asks whether future members of the Supreme Court should themselves be appointed to the House of Lords upon their retirement, citing their *"significant contribution"* to legislative work. We are wary of this for two reasons. Firstly, such a question is evidence of the Government's expectation (not simply its desire) of the future composition of the House of Lords; it does not countenance the possibility that the House might be fully elected, either directly or by an indirect system such as 'secondary mandate.'[85] Whilst the subject is outside of our remit, we believe that there is force in the arguments for an all-elected model.

Secondly, the Government has elsewhere suggested that retired members of the Supreme Court might form part of the court's reserve list for their first five years of retirement.[86] For them to remain as judges, albeit infrequently, at the same time as sitting as legislators would defeat much of the object of creating a Supreme Court in the first place. Therefore, if they were to remain on a reserve list for five years after their retirement, they could not rightly be appointed to the House of Lords until the end of that period. As the proposed retirement age for members of the Supreme Court is 75 years,[87] it is questionable whether many would have the will or the energy to make a significant contribution to Parliamentary work once they were appointed to the Lords half a decade later. As we discussed earlier,[88] there are individuals with eminent legal expertise outside the judiciary who could in that situation – and already do – provide the House with a comparable service in scrutinising proposed legislation.

---

85 For an explanation of 'secondary mandate', see Billy Bragg, *A People's Second Chamber, The Guardian,* 5th November 2001.

86 *Constitutional Reform: A Supreme Court for the United Kingdom* (Department for Constitutional Affairs, July 2003), p.36.

87 See p, 74.

88 See p.48.

However, if – as we propose – the new Supreme Court were to have only full-time members, with no reserve list, this objection to former members' appointment to the House of Lords evaporates. In that event, if the House were to remain at least in part appointed, we would support a convention that retiring members were given a peerage. Their contributions to scrutinising proposed legislation, whilst perhaps over-exaggerated by some in terms of their uniqueness,[89] would nonetheless prove a highly valuable asset.

Over the past years, the retirement age for law lords has been whittled down from 75 to 70. A return to 75 has been mooted by the Government in its consultation paper.[90] This would seem a desirable change. The nature of a judge's career means that a member of the highest court would not normally be appointed before he had reached an age at which many professional people would be thinking of retiring; therefore, this higher retirement age for Supreme Court members would allow for some stability and continuity in the court. The example of Lord Denning, who, exceptionally, continued to sit as a senior judge until the age of 83, illustrates that old age need not detract from judges' ability to perform their jobs.

Administration and Budget

The Senior Law Lord

The Senior Law Lord is effectively the president of the Appellate Committee. He represents the court on official occasions and presides over the panel on which he is sitting, in which capacity he allocates responsibility for writing judgments. The Deputy Senior Law Lord presides over any other simultaneous panel. Most importantly, the

---

89   See p, 48.
90   *Constitutional Reform: A Supreme Court for the United Kingdom* (Department for Constitutional Affairs, July 2003), p.36.

Senior Law Lord and his Deputy are responsible for approving listing arrangements for each legal term;[91] because the Appellate Committee and Judicial Committee do not sit *en banc*, this responsibility carries with it the choice as to which judges should hear each case – a discretion which may have the power to influence outcomes, whether intentionally or not.[92] These functions have in theory been delegated to the Senior Law Lord by the Lord Chancellor; after the proposed abolition of the Lord Chancellor and the Appellate Committee have taken place, a President of the Supreme Court is to take over the Senior Law Lord's role in his own right.[93] In light of his important powers, it is important to consider how the President should be selected.[94]

The convention that the office of Senior Law Lord was automatically assumed by the longest serving law lord was altered by the Government in 1984. The position has since been appointed by the executive, following the selection process for law lords and judges generally: the Lord Chancellor puts a list of names to the Prime Minister who then recommends a candidate to the Queen, who makes the appointment. The consultation paper on the Supreme Court asks whether, once Lord Bingham has retired from the office, future Presidents of the Supreme Court should continue to be appointed by the executive or be selected by the proposed Judicial Appointments Commission.[95]

---

91 Along with the senior official responsible for judicial business in the House of Lords (the 'Fourth Clerk of the Table (Judicial)') and his opposite number in the Judicial Committee (the 'Registrar of the Privy Council').

92 See Le Sueur and Cornes, *The Future of the United Kingdom's Highest Courts* (The Constitution Unit, 2001), p.138.

93 *Constitutional Reform: A Supreme Court for the United Kingdom* (Department for Constitutional Affairs, July 2003), p.25.

94 Additionally, we recommend in Chapter Four that the President of the Supreme Court should be on of the nine members of the Judicial Appointments Commission. See p.128.

95 *Constitutional Reform: A Supreme Court for the United Kingdom* (Department for Constitutional Affairs, July 2003), p.25. The Government has rightly suggested that Lord Bingham, as the present Senior Law Lord, will automatically become the first President of the Supreme Court.

Our view is that the former option should not be chosen. If – as is set to happen – the court system is to be restructured in the name of judicial independence, then it would seem contradictory for the Government to retain the ability to handpick the individual who decides which judges sit on any given case. Lord Hailsham's argument in 1984 for empowering the executive to select the Senior Law Lord was that it brought about consistency with the process for judicial appointments.[96] Since judges are now to be selected by a Judicial Appointments Commission, that same consistency would require the appointment of the President to follow suit. Nor is Government influence necessary in order to meet Lord Diplock's incontrovertible assertions that the president of a court must be an efficient administrator as well as an excellent judge, that the two skills do not always go hand in hand, and that administrative efficiency can be inversely proportionate to seniority.[97] The Judicial Appointments Commission would surely be just as capable of acknowledging this.

Another alternative to the President being selected by the Government, which has not been mentioned in the consultation paper, would be for the decision to be left to the judges themselves. As Le Sueur and Cornes point out, this approach may *"enhance the position of the senior judge, as he or she would have the explicit endorsement of their colleagues."*[98] Such a model would not be without precedent – it is the current practice of the Spanish *Tribunal Constitucional*. It would certainly be preferable to executive influence, and it is regrettable that the idea has escaped the Government's attention.

As for the selection of the Deputy President, we see much force in the argument that *"to avoid the presumption that she or he would necessarily*

---

96   H.L. Debs., col. 915-918, 27 June 1984.
97   See Le Sueur and Cornes, *The Future of the United Kingdom's Highest Courts* (The Constitution Unit, 2001), p.130.
98   Le Sueur and Cornes, *The Future of the United Kingdom's Highest Courts* (The Constitution Unit, 2001), p.134.

subsequently be appointed President, that position could continue to be filled as now, by the next most senior member of the Court."[99] This advantage, coupled with the existence of a President chosen specifically for his administrative efficiency, would seem to outweigh the contention that the longest serving judge might not make the most effective Deputy President.

The Supreme Court's budget

The issue of how the new Supreme Court is to be funded escaped attention in most quarters during the aftermath of the Government's proposals for reform. The Government's consultation paper indicates that funding of the Court is to come from the budget of the new Department for Constitutional Affairs. In fact, this is an important change: the Appellate Committee's status as part of the legislature means that it is currently funded out of the Parliament budget, not the Treasury budget. Moreover, the DCA appears set to be a far more 'political' department than its predecessor, the Lord Chancellor's Department.[100] As Lord Lester of Herne Hill QC stressed to us, the danger is that political cost-cutting exercises will hamper the resources available to, and therefore the efficiency of, the Supreme Court. Yet the paucity of resources available under the present system is one of the prime reasons for creating a Supreme Court in the first place! As Richard Cornes has explained, many countries safeguard against this danger by 'ringfencing' their courts' budget:

> *"Ideally, from the point of view of securing a supreme court's independence from the other branches, and in fact commonly, supreme courts are given the responsibility for preparing their own budget which is then include a single line in the annual government budget."*[101]

---

99   Cornes, *Constitutional Reform: A Supreme Court for the United Kingdom* (forthcoming article).
100 See Chapter Three, *passim.*
101 Cornes, *Constitutional Reform: A Supreme Court for the United Kingdom* (forthcoming article).

If the funding of the Supreme Court is indeed to come out of the Department for Constitutional Affairs' budget, other safeguards should be set in place. In particular, instead of having DCA officials running the Court, the judges should be allowed to appoint their own Chief Executive, who could then select staff from the general civil service. The Court should also, under this model, draft its own budget for inclusion as a single line in the DCA's budget; the Chief Executive and the President of the Court could then appear before the appropriate Parliamentary Select Committee to answer questions on it.[102]

Accessibility to the public

> *"Above all, …the Supreme Court must be modern. Legislation should allow for the proceedings to be televised. Hearings should be live on the internet and papers filed by the parties should generally be made available online. These are exciting times. If we fail to build a Supreme Court worthy of the name, we may have to wait another 130 years for a second chance."* – Joshua Rozenberg[103]

As we have already noted, public confidence in the judiciary in Britain is markedly low, compared to both other nations' perceptions of judges and domestic opinions of other professions. We agree with Mr Rozenberg that, in setting up the Supreme Court, the opportunity should be taken to increase the openness and accessibility of the highest court. Televised hearings, so long as they respect the privacy of litigants, would be a positive step – not least because our common law system means that judges themselves can make laws that have an important influence on the way we run our lives.[104]

---

102   As suggested by Cornes, *Constitutional Reform: A Supreme Court for the United Kingdom* (forth-coming article).
103   Joshua Rozenberg, *The Daily Telegraph*, 26th July 2003.
104   See pp.130–131

Other means should be adopted to increase openness at the apex of justice. As JUSTICE has recently observed:

> *"Many Supreme Courts around the world have guided tours and public information programmes. This is not merely window dressing, it plays an important role in enhancing public understanding of, and confidence in, the legal system."*[105]

Such guided tours would be welcome. It could also be argued that the Supreme Court itself should go on circuit so as to improve accessibility to justice. However, this seems a step too far; the expense and adverse effect on the Court's efficiency would outweigh the benefits of such a move. It might also be thought that the highest court requires the austerity of a single, recognisable building. Besides, the United Kingdom jurisdiction covers a relatively small geographical area; London is easily reached from most parts in only a few hours at a reasonable price.

Wider Implications of Reform

Other judges who hold peerages

The Appellate Committee is not the only court to contain members who are both judges and legislators. It is customary for the Lord Chief Justice and the Master of the Rolls, who sit full-time in the Court of Appeal, to be appointed to the House of Lords upon taking up office. The consultation paper issued by the Department for Constitutional Affairs asks whether this arrangement should cease.[106] The answer must be yes: the arguments in favour of removing the law lords from the

---

105   *A Supreme Court for the United Kingdom* (JUSTICE Briefing Paper, May 2003), p.5.
106   *Constitutional Reform: A Supreme Court for the United Kingdom* (Department for Constitutional Affairs, July 2003), p.27.

legislature apply equally to these other judges; any inconsistent application of these arguments would detract from the benefits – and the credibility – of the proposed reforms.

Legislators who sit as recorders

A small number of legally-qualified MPs undertake part-time judicial work as recorders. Prima facie, they would seem to be threatened by the arguments in favour of removing the law lords from Parliament. Public comments by a recorder in a legal magazine have already formed the basis of a successful challenge to his decision on the same issue.[107] Ross Cranston QC MP, who himself sits both as a legislator in the House of Commons and as a recorder, acknowledged that the issue was a live one:

> *"I'm sure us sitting as MPs and Recorders will be in the firing line at some stage; taking the theory and applying it logically."*

Dr Kate Malleson also saw the potential threat to the dual role of MP-recorders, but made clear that the case against judges sitting as legislators need not necessarily have the same weight at every level:

> *"It's much better for us to look at each individual circumstance. You have to say, does this job conflict with that? Is there a vested interest here that could be problematic, both in theory and in practice? And then you've got to ask yourself, what's the benefit that we get from it?*

Whilst the advantages of having law lords within Parliament are limited – they cannot offer expert advice on legislation without jeopardising their objective impartiality and the purported benefits that they enjoy

---

107   *Timmins v Gormley* [2000] 2 W.L.R. 870 (CA).

from observing the legislative process from within are available from other sources – Paul Stinchcombe MP explained to us that MP-recorders benefited themselves as legislators (which, unlike the law lords, is their primary role) and brought certain advantages to the House of Commons as a whole:

> *"What they actually do bring to the legislative process is an experience of what actually happens in that part of the real world – it's not a matter of putting legal submissions in the House of Lords, it's what a seventeen year-old who has thrown a brick through a window says when he's in court – real every day issues like this. That perhaps is a level of exposure that's good for legislators."*

The 'constitutional clarification' arguments in favour of removing the highest court from the House of Lords have much less force vis-à-vis MPs who sit as part-time recorders. There are only twelve law lords, who make up the most senior and high profile court in the country; *all* of them currently sit within the legislature. Conversely, there are 1,342 recorders,[108] of which all but a mere handful have no place within Parliament. Thus, on a cost-benefit balance, it would seem that a ban on MPs and members of the House of Lords sitting as recorders is undesirable.

Judges chairing public inquiries
In 2001, two highly respected publications expressed concern at the use of law lords to chair important public inquiries.[109] One of them has suggested that they might be replaced altogether in this role by senior civil servants, academics and former judges.[110]

---

108 As at 1ˢᵗ January 2003 – see: *Judicial Statistics 2002* (Department for Constitutional Affairs, 2003), p.95.

109 Woodhouse, *The Office of Lord Chancellor* (Hart Publishing, 2001), p.33; Le Sueur and Cornes, *The Future of the United Kingdom's Highest Courts* (The Constitution Unit, 2001), pp.144-145.

110 Who already chair some inquiries: Le Sueur and Cornes, *Future of the United Kingdom's Highest Courts* (The Constitution Unit, 2001), p.144. Lord Lester of Herne Hill QC expressed agreement with this proposal in his interview with us.

The first reason given for this is that taking members of the highest court away from their primary role of hearing legal cases only serves to accentuate the increasing backlog of cases awaiting hearing.[111] However, this objection is not decisive. It may well be that, after the creation of a fully-resourced Supreme Court, the backlog currently facing the Appellate Committee diminishes, the effective administration of justice no longer being hampered by inadequate facilities. If the occasional absence of a Supreme Court member really will be a problem, then the number of the Court's members could be increased to, say, fourteen.[112]

More convincing is the argument that *"while [judges] give an aura of independence to the [inquiry] process, there is a danger that the process itself will be seen as political..., casting doubt on their independence."*[113] For example, in 1996, when Sir Richard Scott's report into the Matrix Churchill affair criticised certain officials and ministers, he was subjected to a whispering campaign in Whitehall and Westminster, which sought to undermine its findings and his integrity. After Sir Richard defended his report, he was accused of being "anti-government" and thus, by implication, of not retaining the independence and objectivity required of him as a judge.[114]

However, Lord Justice Laws pointed out an equally weighty argument in favour of retaining top judges' availability to chair the most important inquiries: for certain inquiries of overwhelming importance, the public will demand a chairman of the standing, profile and independence that only a senior sitting judge can provide.

Both these arguments are weighty; it is difficult to choose between the two. On balance, we would not discontinue their availability for important inquiries; we feel that the benefit to the public of having a

---

112   Le Sueur and Cornes, *Future of the United Kingdom's Highest Courts* (The Constitution Unit, 2001), p.144. For a statistical analysis of the backlog, See p. 42.
113   See pp.65–67.
114   Woodhouse, *The Office of Lord Chancellor* (Hart Publishing, 2001), p.33.
115   *ibid.*

sitting senior judge chairing inquiries of fundamental importance outweighs the burden of having that judge thrust into the political limelight for a few months. However, the choice of which judge should chair an inquiry should not rest with the Government (as it did, for example, with the Hutton inquiry), but with the Judicial Appointments Commission discussed in Chapter Four. This modification, coupled with the other proposed reforms to enshrine judicial independence from the legislature and executive, could then be highlighted by judges to counter allegations of their non-independence by parties criticised in their inquiry reports.

3. Reforming the Office of the Lord Chancellor

Introduction

The office of Lord Chancellor is ancient: it has existed *"nearly as long as the monarchy and longer than Parliament."*[1] The precise date of its foundation is uncertain: some put it in the seventh century,[2] although most constitutional historians prefer the eleventh century as the official starting point.[3] The evolution of the office from its ecclesiastical and administrative beginnings into its current form is highly complicated;[4] for present purposes it will suffice to observe that the Lord Chancellor took on a judicial role in the fourteenth century,[5] was formally recognised as the presiding officer of the House of Lords in 1539,[6] became known as the

1   Woodhouse, *The Office of Lord Chancellor* (Hart Publishing, 2001), p.1.

2   The first holder of the office was Andgmendus in 605AD, according to the old LCD website and Lord MacKay, *The Lord Chancellor in the 1990s* (1991) 44 *Current Legal Problems* 241.

3   See Underhill, *The Lord Chancellor* (Terence Dalton, 1978) p.1; Sir William Anson, *The Law and Custom of the Constitution*, Vol II, Part 1 (4th edn, Clarendon Press, 1935).

4   An detailed account is given in Woodhouse, *The Office of Lord Chancellor,* (Hart Publishing, 2001), pp.1-12.

5   Underhill, *The Lord Chancellor*, (Terence Dalton, 1978), p.75.

6   *ibid.* p.102.

head of the judiciary around two centuries later,[7] and emerged as a head of a government department at the end of the nineteenth century.[8]

Today, the Lord Chancellor has four main functions. He is a senior Cabinet Minister, in charge of a high spending government department; he acts as Speaker of the House of Lords; he is head of the judiciary in England and Wales; he is responsible for appointing judges and QCs; and he sits – albeit infrequently – as presiding judge in the Appellate Committee of the House of Lords.

The Government's approach to reform

As with the other proposals for judicial reform, the Government's sudden announcement that it intended the office of the Lord Chancellor to be abolished ought not to have been made without any prior consultation. Such important constitutional change should rightly be the product of detailed consideration and a wide consensus. By contrast, even the Government itself seemed uncertain of the immediate effects of its decision: hence Lord Falconer's initial declaration that he would not sit as speaker of the House of Lords, followed by his later realisation that he would have to do so until peers decided upon his replacement.[9]

> "The idea that there could have been serious input by civil servants, as there should have been into proposals of these kinds, is nonsensical. They couldn't even identify the X million times the Lord Chancellor is referred to in statute, and they hadn't dealt with the need for him to sit on the Woolsack. If a student submitted a paper like this as an essay to you or I, we'd say "go away and do it again!" I know enough of our civil service to know they weren't involved in putting this together. When people say this was drawn up on the back of an envelope, it's probably because it was drawn up on an envelope." – **Michael Beloff QC**

7   Lord Hailsham, *A Sparrow's Flight* (Collins, 1990) p.379.
8   See Woodhouse, *The Office of Lord Chancellor* (Hart Publishing, 2001), p.6.
9   On June 12th, the Downing Street website said that Lord Falconer would *"not fulfil either the judicial function of Lord Chancellor or the role of speaker."* The next day, Lord Falconer realised his mistake and was forced to sit on the woolsack as Speaker of the House of Lords.

However, the fact that the announcement came out of the blue does not mean that the substantive policy behind it was necessarily unthinkable or ill advised – a charge levied by certain parties in the days following 12th June 2003.[10] The office of Lord Chancellor had for many years been criticised in many quarters. Recent proponents of reform include academics,[11] at least one law lord[12] and campaign groups.[13] Michael Beloff QC encapsulated the reaction of many:

> *"It was inevitable in the end that the change had to come. I'd prefer it to have gone out for consultation first, but that's methodology rather than ends."*

In Chapters Four and Five, we support the termination of the Lord Chancellor's unfettered discretion over the appointment of judges and QCs. This Chapter shall evaluate the arguments for and against abolishing the Lord Chancellor's other roles. We shall initially deal the aspects of his office which have raised the most objections: his functions as a judge, as head of the judiciary and as an unelected Cabinet minister. Consideration shall then be given as to whether, if these features were to be removed, the recent calls for retaining the title of Lord Chancellor for the Speaker of the House of Lords are viable.

Problems with the Lord Chancellor's Judicial Functions

The Lord Chancellor as a judge

Chapter One of this book has already detailed the objections to legisla-

---

10 In particular, the Conservative Party leadership. See, *eg.* H.C. Debs., col. 358, 18th June 2003.
11 See *eg.* Woodhouse, *The Office of Lord Chancellor* (Hart Publishing, 2001).
12 Lord Steyn, *The Weakest and Least Dangerous Department of Government* [1997] P.L. 84, and *The Case for a Supreme Court* (2001) 118 L.Q.R. 382.
13 JUSTICE, *The Judicial Functions of the House of Lords* (Written Evidence to the Royal Commission on the Reform of the House of Lords, May 1999); Spencer, *Time for a Ministry of Justice?* (Institute for Public Policy Research, 2001).

tors sitting as judges; it will suffice to repeat here that they are of enough weight to require there to be strong arguments in favour of retaining the dual function, which in the case of the law lords we conclude that there are not. These problems apply no less to the Lord Chancellor, but with an added dimension: as well as being a legislator, the Lord Chancellor is also a member of the executive, a Cabinet Minister. This conveys an overtly political aspect that the law lords do not have – and, as an authoritative book by Prof. Woodhouse demonstrated in 2001, his role has become more and more 'politicised' in recent years.[14]

"He is responsible for formulating and implementing policies affecting the administration of justice, which are often a matter of party political debate. In addition he chairs Cabinet committees over a large range of policy issues beyond his departmental responsibility. His is at the centre of political power in a party political sense. In all these respects he is bound by the doctrine of collective responsibility." – **Lord Steyn**[15]

Moreover, unlike other senior judges, the appointment and tenure of Lord Chancellors depends on the executive: they are party political appointments, they *"hold office for reasons of their loyalty to the government of the day,"*[16] and they can be dismissed if they incur the Prime Minister's displeasure – as Lord Irvine himself discovered!

The Lord Chancellor's position vis-à-vis Article 6(1) ECHR and objective impartiality is consequently even more precarious than that of the law lords.[17] As was written in a leading article on *McGonnell v United Kingdom*, when one of the law lords publicly states that the Lord Chancellor *"is always a spokesman for the government in furtherance of*

---

14   Woodhouse, *The Office of Lord Chancellor*, (Hart Publishing, 2001), p.13.
15   Lord Steyn, *The Case for a Supreme Court* (2001) 118 L.Q.R. 382, at p.384.
16   Cornes and Le Sueur, *The Future of the United Kingdom's Highest Courts*, (The Constitution Unit, 2001), p.132.
17   See pp.25–35

its own agenda,"[18] can a reasonable onlooker have no doubt at all as to his judicial impartiality in cases involving the executive's interests?[19]

> "A Lord Chancellor's connection to the executive could give rise to an appearance of partiality in any case in which the government might be said to have an interest." – **Richard Cornes**[20]

Put in terms of the rule of law, this notion of a Cabinet Minister sitting as a judge is also more objectionable than the dual functions of the law lords. Unlike legislative inroads into the rule of law, *ultra vires* executive acts can always be prevented or remedied by the courts, meaning that judicial independence from the executive is even more important than judicial independence from the legislature.[21] This is not a purely theoretical problem: it carries the practical danger of undermining public confidence in the judiciary, which empirical evidence illustrates is low.[22] As Lord Steyn has recently written:

"It is of paramount importance that the nation must have confidence in judges at every level as independent and impartial guardians of the rule of law. What must citizens make of the fact that in the highest court a member of the Government participates in judicial decision making? Surely it creates a risk of undermining in public perception the belief that our highest court is a neutral and impartial arbiter in our affairs?"[23]

---

18 Lord Steyn, *The Weakest and Least Dangerous Department of Government* [1997] P.L. 84, at 90-1.
19 Cornes, *McGonnell v United Kingdom, the Lord Chancellor and the Law Lords* (2000) P.L. 166, at p.174. (see also p.169), emphasising that even on less strict interpretations of Article 6(1) (such of that of Sir John Laws in *McGonnell*) than those repeatedly issued by the European Court of Human Rights, the Lord Chancellor would most probably be in breach (sometimes even under the *subjective* test) when hearing cases that have implications for the executive.
20 Cornes, *McGonnell v United Kingdom, the Lord Chancellor and the Law Lords* (2000) P.L. 166, at p.175
21 Inroads into the rule of law by Parliament cannot be remedied by overturning an Act of Parliament, but can only by watered down through principles of statutory interpretation. See pp. 35–37
22 See p. 51.
23 Lord Steyn, *The Case for a Supreme Court* (2001) 118 L.Q.R. 382, at p.389.

An excellent example of these problems is the case of *Pepper v Hart*.[24] Here, one party sought the introduction of a new common law rule of statutory construction whereby, in certain circumstances, judges could refer to *Hansard* records of what was said in Parliamentary debates, in order to interpret ambiguous legislative provisions. The majority of the Appellate Committee agreed to such a move, but the sitting Lord Chancellor, Lord MacKay, who was one of the judges in the case, dissented on public policy grounds:

> *"Such an approach appears to me to involve the possibility at least of an immense increase of the cost in litigation in which statutory construction is involved. It is of course easy to overestimate such cost but it is I fear equally easy to underestimate it.... Your Lordships are well aware that the costs of litigation are a subject of general public concern and I personally would not wish to be a party to changing a well established rule which could have a substantial effect in increasing these costs.... I would certainly be prepared to agree the rule should no longer be adhered to were it not for the practical consideration to which I have referred."*[25]

In his ministerial capacity, Lord Mackay had adopted an overt policy of cutting public expenditure in the courts, which had itself aroused significant antagonism from the judiciary, who perceived him as putting the concerns of the executive before the interests of justice.[26] Therefore, his opposition to the legal submission in *Pepper v Hart* on the sole basis of the potential increase in the cost of litigation raises considerable doubt as to whether his judicial decision in that case was

---

24   *Pepper (Inspector of Taxes) v Hart* [1993] A.C. 593.
25   *Ibid.*, at p. 615.
26   See Spencer, *Time for a Ministry of Justice?* (Institute for Public Policy Research, 2001), p.12; Woodhouse, *The Office of Lord Chancellor* (Hart Publishing, 2001), *in passim*.

made totally without the interests of the executive in mind. Michael Beloff QC commented:

"You've got someone saying "wait a minute, this is going to cost a lot of money." I think that's actually what he did think. At the very least, it's easy for people to say: "that's Treasury-driven, it's not just an objective view of the material before him.""

This is by no means an isolated example: more recently, the first two cases on which Lord Irvine sat involved the relationship between the executive and citizens[27]. On more than one occasion, he withdrew at the last minute from hearing a case due to threats by litigants' lawyers of an Article 6(1) challenge.[28]

Lord Irvine later said that he would not sit in cases involving human rights challenges or cases *"where interests of the executive are directly engaged."*[29] However, this did not eliminate the problem. Firstly, it was a mere personal statement; the pattern of the office of Lord Chancellor, including under Lord Irvine's reign, told a different story. There were no guarantees for the future; as Lord Irvine himself insisted in 1999, there are no constitutional conventions governing the participation of the Lord Chancellor in judicial business.[30] *"He asserts an absolute right in his unfettered discretion when to sit."*[31] Secondly, the

---

27   *Boddington v British Transport Police* [1999] 2 AC 143 and *Director of Public Prosecutions v Jones* [1999] 2 AC 240. In the latter case, Lord Irvine's vote was decisive, as the Appellate Committee was split 3-2. His role in both cases was criticised at the time in the House Lords by Lord Lester of Herne Hill [*Hansard*, H.L. Deb., October 28, 1988, col. 197].

28   See Rachel Sylvester, *Irvine Withdraws from Sitting as a Judge in the Lords*, The Daily Telegraph, 21st February 2001.

29   In his speech to the Worldwide Conference of Common Law Judges, 5th July 1999, reiterated in an interview with *The Times* - Frances Gibb, *More Judges Needed for Rights Challenges*, The Times, 7th September 1999.

30   See *Hansard*, H.L. Deb., June 22, 1999, written answers, cols. 77-78, where Lord Irvine rejected the idea that he should follow the advice of the Senior Law Lord or Law Lords collectively about his sitting.

31   Lord Steyn, *The Case for a Supreme Court* (2001) 118 L.Q.R. 382, at p.386.

Lord Chancellor's highly party-political role means that problems of objective impartiality are not limited to cases directly affecting the executive; it accentuates the problems associated with legislators sitting as judges, as discussed in Chapter One. In any case, it is difficult to draw the line between cases where 'the executive's interests are engaged' and cases where they are not. What if *Pepper v Hart* had been a case between two private parties, but with the same issue of statutory construction at stake?[32] The executive would have no *legal* interest in the case, but only a *political* interest – namely, public policy concerns over increased expenditure in litigation if a new common law rule of statutory construction were to be allowed. Would this be enough for the case to have 'directly engaged the executive's interests'? If not, then the objective impartiality problems do not go away: the Lord Chancellor would still have sat under Lord Irvine's guideline. If so, then there are hardly any cases on which the guideline could permit the Lord Chancellor to sit, since there are public policy questions with party-political dimensions at stake in hordes of cases between private parties.

Indeed, Lord Irvine's assurances were not enough to prevent his overlapping functions being condemned in April 2003 by a key committee of the Council of Europe, the 44-nation body which oversees the operation of the European Convention on Human Rights, in April 2003. Following a report by Professor Erik Jurgens,[33] the Committee on Legal Affairs and Human Rights unanimously endorsed a draft resolution, recommending the United Kingdom to cease the Lord Chancellor's role as a judge, on Article 6(1) grounds. Professor Jurgens' report has rightly been criticised for overplaying the role of 'separation of powers' as a British constitutional

---

32   As it happened, one of the litigants in this case was an executive official.
33   A constitutional law academic from the Netherlands and Rapporteur of the Committee on Legal Affairs and Human Rights, Parliamentary Assembly, Council of Europe.

principle,[34] but the very endorsement of the resolution by the Committee further demonstrates that Lord Irvine's personal statement in 1999 was by no means the end of the matter in ECHR terms.

Another problem arising out of the law lords' dual role may have even greater weight with regard to the Lord Chancellor sitting as a judge: that, in these days of spreading democratic values across the globe, the United Kingdom is open to charges of hypocrisy.[35] In a recent debate on the proposed judicial reforms, Baroness Kennedy spoke of her experience of accompanying, in her capacity as Chair of the British Council, the President of the Supreme Court of Russia to meet our senior judiciary:[36]

> *"The British Council had been engaged in assisting a programme of law reform in Russia, including the drafting of legislation to underpin the independence of the judiciary. As Chair of the British Council, I went with Justice Lebedev to meet the Lord Chancellor. On the way, he and I have a lively discussion about the importance of an independent judiciary and how crucial it was to a vibrant democracy.... He explained how hard it was to persuade the Russian public, after years of political control, that the judges really were independent and that they could be trusted. But he then with a twinkle asked me to explain how our system worked, with our Lord Chancellor wearing three hats. I have to say that I rather wickedly in return suggested that he ask the Lord Chancellor... [Lord Irvine's] explanation was all about tradition and Chinese*

---

34   In particular, by Ross Cranston QC MP in his interview with us and during his questioning of Professor Jurgens at the Select Committee on the Lord Chancellor's Department, 27th March 2003. Professor Jurgens appears to rely on the *institutional* separation of powers as a constitutional principle – yet there is no such constitutional principle in Britain. For an explanation of how 'separation of powers' does apply to this debate, See pp. 35–37

35   See pp. 37–39.

36   HL Debs. 8th September 2003.

walls, all of which sounded half-baked to a reform-minded Russian, who would be meeting senior judges from Czechoslovakia and other countries that wanted to apply to belong to the Council of Europe, all of whom were seeking to make their judiciary more independent."

> "Every day in my Council of Europe work I am in confrontation with new democracies from Central and Eastern Europe, whom I tell that they should not do certain things [that undermine judicial independence], and they say: "what about the British?"" – **Professor Erik Jurgens**[37]

There are further concerns over the fact that the Lord Chancellor need not have held any prior judicial office.[38] Lord Irvine's career on the Bench before 1997 consisted of a few years as a mere part-time Recorder and Deputy High Court Judge. Yet his colleagues on the Appellate Committee, the Lords of Appeal in Ordinary, are the top twelve of over a thousand judges, who in turn have been selected from more than thirteen thousand barristers and other legal professionals.[39] With only a handful of exceptions, all law lords have risen up through the judicial ranks, since it is thought that even the best legal minds require full-time experience as judges before being fully suited to sitting in the country's highest court – just as even the most talented footballer would not be appointed as Manager of the England team without gaining managerial experience at club level. Unless there are arguments in favour of such a judicial novice sitting as a law lord, this would seem contrary to the public interest, in terms of both the actual and the perceived calibre of the highest court.

---

37   Evidence to the Select Committee on the Lord Chancellor's Department, 27th March 2002.
38   See Woodhouse, *The Office of Lord Chancellor*, (Hart Publishing, 2001), p.12.
39   The total number of Lord Justices of Appeal, High Court Judges, Circuit Judges and District Judges in 2000-2001 was 1112 [*Court Service Plan*, 2000-2003]. The total number of practising barristers in 2002 was 13,601 [*Bar Council Statistics*, December 2002].

The Lord Chancellor as head of the judiciary

> "The notion that a government minister should be head of the judiciary would seem to undermine, rather than protect, judicial independence." – **Professor Woodhouse**[40]

As well as sitting as a judge, the Lord Chancellor is also head of the judiciary in England and Wales and Northern Ireland. This role is not purely symbolic and ceremonial: he is the judges' representative, responsible for channelling their concerns and guarding against threats to their independence, through public speeches and private representations.[41] Strong objections have been made as to the compatibility of this function with the Lord Chancellor's role as a senior member of the executive and a highly party-political figure:

"The executive and the judges are not on the same side. Their functions, duties and perspectives are different. Inevitably there are sometimes tensions between the executive and judiciary..... How then can a Cabinet Minister be a spokesman for the judges? Threats to judicial independence rarely come from citizens. Rather they come from a government irked by the judiciary fulfilling its traditional role of standing between the executive and the citizen....It is therefore curious for the Lord Chancellor to be the spokesman on behalf of the judges.."[42]

At the very least, this can cause confusion in determining when the Lord Chancellor is speaking as a Cabinet Minister and when he is speaking as head of the judiciary, particularly when he is replying to

---

40   Woodhouse, *The Office of Lord Chancellor*, (Hart Publishing, 2001), p.12.
41   He is also in charge of dealing with complaints against judges and disciplining those at Circuit judge level and below.
42   Lord Steyn, *The Case for a Supreme Court* (2001) 118 L.Q.R. 382, at p.394.

debates in the House of Lords.[43] It is difficult for the public to realise by which branch of government ideas and policies are being put forward, and to judge them accordingly – as is their democratic right.

Worse still, there have on an increasingly frequent number of occasions been legitimate concerns that that individual Lord Chancellors have given their executive, party-political role greater weight than their responsibilities as head of the judiciary.

> "Most people in the judicial profession would consider that over the last few years we've had more of the Lord Chancellor speaking for the government to the judiciary – cutting expenditure and so on – than for the judiciary to government." – **Michael Beloff QC**

In 1997, when Lord Irvine spoke to the judges for the first time, he criticised the former Conservative Government, accusing John Major of *"complacency"* and *"enervating insularity,"* whilst praising New Labour in no uncertain terms.[44] *"Surely, the Lord Chancellor was not speaking as head of the judiciary."*[45] In 1994, Lord Chancellor Mackay sought to persuade the President of the Employment Appeals Tribunal, Mr Justice Wood, to review the appeal procedure he had adopted, for reasons of efficiency and cost effectiveness. In the resulting debate in the House of Lords, concern was expressed that the principle that a judge has complete discretion in his own court was being eroded, thereby posing a threat to judicial independence. *"Moreover, the anxiety was heightened by the fact that the threat came from the person charged with protecting that independence and it appeared to arise from a conflict between his executive and constitutional roles."*[46] This is not, however, a

---

43   Woodhouse, *The Office of Lord Chancellor* (Hart Publishing, 2001), p.8.
44   Lord Irvine of Lairg, Speech to HM Judges, Mansion House, July 23rd 1997.
45   Lord Steyn, *The Case for a Supreme Court* (2001) 118 L.Q.R. 382, at p.395.
46   Woodhouse, *The Office of Lord Chancellor*, (Hart Publishing, 2001), p.33.

purely recent phenomenon. For example, over fifty years ago, Lord Jowitt LC wrote to the Lord Chief Justice, Lord Goddard, expressing the hope that *"the judges will not be lenient on those bandits* [who] *carry arms* [to] *shoot at the police."*[47] Whilst we cannot know how much influence this pressure had, it is noteworthy that two years later Derek Bentley was sentenced to death by Lord Goddard himself, in what was later considered an overly harsh decision.

Moreover, in circumstances where the independence of the judiciary is threatened by a particular act or utterance by another minister, the doctrine of collective Cabinet responsibility and the classified status of Cabinet minutes mean that the Lord Chancellor is prevented from speaking out in public against his colleague on behalf of the judiciary that he heads. So, in early 2003, when prompted by the Select Committee on the Lord Chancellor's Department to detail how he has defended judicial independence within Cabinet, Lord Irvine responded:

"Obviously I am not at liberty to talk about discussions which take place in Cabinet and obviously I am bound by collective responsibility."[48]

Since 2001, judges of cases lost by the Home Office have repeatedly been criticised by Home Secretary Blunkett.[49] On not one occasion did the Lord Chancellor publicly rise to their defence.[50] With an ever-

---

47   In 1947: LCO 2/3830, quoted in Stevens, *The Independence of the Judiciary* (Clarendon Press, 1997), p.95.

48   Minutes of the Select Committee on the Lord Chancellor's Department, 2nd April 2003.

49   Joshua Rozenberg, *The Daily Telegraph,* November 11, 2001.

50   His only public remark, which was not in response to any specific utterance or proposal by Mr Blunkett, was a very general comment to a Select Committee, nearly two years after the Home Secretary's attacks began: *"When the judiciary give decisions that the executive doesn't like, as in all governments, some ministers have spoken out against some decisions that they don't like. I disapprove of that. I think it undermines the rule of law and I think that maturity requires that when you get a decision that favours you, you do not clap and when you get one that goes against you, you don't boo."* [Minutes of the Select Committee on the LCD, 2nd April 2003].

aggressive media increasingly interested in judges' work,[51] such attacks can only serve to undermine public confidence in the judiciary, unless its head is someone who is entirely free to defend it in full force in the public domain.

These anecdotes – and they are by no means the only ones[52] – demonstrate that concerns about the Lord Chancellor's role as head of the judiciary are firmly grounded in practice and not purely theoretical, as proponents of the status quo tend to argue.

Too much of a job for one man?

A further argument for ending the Lord Chancellor's role as a judge and siphoning off his position as head of the judiciary to another senior judge is more simple: the office Lord Chancellor has too many roles for one man to perform. As well as these functions, he runs a high-spending department responsible for the administration of justice, civil law reform, devolution issues, human rights, referenda, freedom of information, royal and Church issues – to name but a few. He also plays an important role in key policy initiatives, such as the Labour Government's ongoing constitutional reform programme. on one view, something had to give. Ross Cranston QC MP told us that he considered this argument to be more decisive than those discussed above; Michael Beloff QC commented that *"having two or three jobs, it's difficult to fit the legal work in with the others."* It would seem that this is one of the Government's own motives for reform, judging by Lord Falconer's assertion that *"the time has come for…a minister able to <u>focus</u> on delivering a better justice system for all."*[53]

---

51   Prompted by interest in the enactment of the Human Rights Act 1998 and the *Pinochet* case (on which, see *e.g.* Harrison, *What Pinochet Has Done for the Law Lords*, (1999) 149 *New Law Journal* 477).

52   See Woodhouse, *The Office of Lord Chancellor*, (Hart Publishing, 2001), p.33.

53   Lord Falconer, speech at the Annual Dinner for HM Judges, Mansion House, 9th July 2003 (emphasis added).

Whilst the Lord Chancellor's executive responsibilities would always have to be performed by a minister, there are obvious candidates to take over his position as head of the judiciary (for example, the Lord Chief Justice) and his absence from the Bench would have little bearing upon the efficiency of the highest court.[54] Therefore, if something had to give – and this seems quite probable – it ought logically to have been those two roles.

Arguments for the Lord Chancellor's Judicial Functions

Preserving judicial independence

Ironically, judicial independence is also cited by proponents of the current system. Lord Hailsham ranked this as the Lord Chancellor's 'paramount duty',[55] famously saying in 1979:

> *"It is the function of the Lord Chancellor to fight, to his last gasp if need be, for the independence of the judiciary. He can perform that function only if he has a foot in all three camps."* [56]

According to this argument, the Lord Chancellor's current powers are justified on the grounds that, as a judge who is also a senior minister, he provides an authoritative voice for judicial independence, capable of influencing other Cabinet ministers in a way that alternative heads of the judiciary could not.[57] One of our consultees, Sir Nicholas Lyell QC, who has considerable experience of the inner workings of Cabinet government, expressed sympathy with this view – as has Lord Woolf,

---

54 Even if it would, an extra Lord of Appeal in Ordinary could always be created in his place.
55 Lord Hailsham of St Marylebone LC, *The Office of Lord Chancellor and the Separation of Powers* (1989) *Civil Justice Quarterly* 308, at p.312.
56 Speech to the Council of Europe, 1979, as quoted in Edward Garnier QC MP, *Good Riddance? The Office of the Lord Chancellor: What is the Government Up To, and Do We Care?*, *Counsel*, July 2003.
57 See William Rees-Mogg, *The Times*, 4th August 2003.

the present Lord Chief Justice.[58] However, we were persuaded by our other consultees that this was an insufficiently forceful argument in favour of the present system.

> "I'm amazed that Harry Woolf is so concerned about this; I don't see why it's necessary to have someone in there. It works without it in other countries." – **Michael Beloff QC**

> "There are other ways of protecting the independence of the judiciary – as in other jurisdictions, where the Chief Justice has to take that role." – **Ross Cranston QC MP**

In no other democracy does the head of the judiciary have *"a foot in all three camps"*; yet judges across the Western world are perfectly capable of communicating to the executive their concerns about threats to judicial independence. Our judiciary is clearly no less able to convey its views:

> *"When after the last election the suggestion was made by Downing Street that supervision of the court system should be transferred to the Home Office the senior judiciary strongly objected. They did so by pointing out that it would be absurd for the Home Office, a regular party before the courts, to control the court system…. The idea was abandoned. The judiciary can and will speak when it is necessary to do so."*[59]

Moreover, in the interests of open and accountable government, it would seem desirable that such communications between the judiciary and executive take place in the public domain – rather than through the conduit of a Lord Chancellor gagged by collective Cabinet responsibility.[60]

---

58   At a media briefing at the High Court on July 31st 2003 – see Clare Dyer, *Woolf Delays Retirement over Reforms*, *The Guardian*, 1st August 2003.
59   Lord Steyn, *The Case for a Supreme Court* (2001) 118 L.Q.R. 382, at p.391.
60   See pp. 97–98 and Woodhouse, *The Office of Lord Chancellor*, (Hart Publishing, 2001), p.21 +

The judiciary's views on more mundane matters such as resources and caseload could also quite easily be conveyed to the Government and to Parliament in the absence of the Lord Chancellor, for example by the laying of an annual report before the appropriate Select Committee.[61]

Therefore, despite Lord Hailsham's seductive rhetoric, his argument that only a three-pronged Lord Chancellor can ensure the independence of the judiciary is unconvincing: logic and hard evidence prove otherwise. This is not surprising: as another former Lord Chancellor has emphasised, his role owes *"nothing to legal doctrine"*[62] – which played no part in its development – and *"far more to history than it does to constitutional principle."*[63]

Besides, whatever advantage there may have been in having a minister responsible for speaking up for judges in Cabinet may well be retained, since the Government has proposed that one of the Secretary of State for Constitutional Affairs' duties, which may be enshrined in statute,[64] will be *"ensuring the independence of the judiciary in England and Wales within Cabinet."*[65] So long as it is made clear that the last word on judicial independence does lie with head of the judiciary, this may provide the best of both worlds.

'The Cabinet has a representative in the judiciary'

Another reason for preserving the Lord Chancellor's tripartite role is said to be that *"the Cabinet has a representative in the judiciary."*[66] According to this line of thought, the presence of a Cabinet minister amongst the judiciary is desirable on the basis he can represent the aims and wishes of the democratically elected government, with regard

---

61 See Le Sueur and Cornes, *The Future of the United Kingdom's Highest Courts* (The Constitution Unit, 2001), p.134.

62 Lord Elwyn-Jones in M. Berlins, *A Man for All Roles*, BBC Radio 4, 9th April 1998.

63 Lord Elwyn-Jones, 'Foreword' in Underhill, *The Lord Chancellor* (Terence Dalton, 1978), p. x.

64 And should be, for the sake of clarity and scrutiny.

65 HL Debs., col. 632, 14th July 2003. See pp/112–115

66 Lord Irvine, evidence to the Select Committee on the Lord Chancellor's Department, 2nd March 2003.

to cases that have important 'political' or public policy aspects, in private discussions with the other judges.

However, the executive has no business at all steering judges' interpretation of the legal limits of its power and/or the development of the common law. To allow otherwise would be to undermine the rule of law.[67] Government policy is not a source of law – the sovereign Parliament is. Should a judgment be delivered that the Government does not like, it can always sponsor legislation which, once it exists as an Act of Parliament, will overrule the court's decision, in accordance with the doctrine of Parliamentary supremacy.

> "If judges are to be informed of policy matters as background relevant to their decisions, it must be done in an open court where the executive's views can be tested in adversarial debate." – Lord Steyn[68]

Similarly, the contention that there is a great benefit to the judiciary *"from the fact that its President is in close touch with current political affairs"*[69] is not decisive. There are plenty of other means through which the judges can – and no doubt do – easily remain abreast of current political and social issues.[70] Indeed, sensitivity to such issues is already a key criterion in the existing scheme for appointments to judicial office, and is likely to become even more so in the future.[71]

Arguments based upon tradition

The Lord Chancellor is an ancient office. Proposals to abolish or fundamentally change it are bound to meet some resistance based upon its

---

67   See pp 35–37 and pp. 89–90
68   Lord Steyn, *The Case for a Supreme Court* (2001) 118 L.Q.R. 382, at p.391.
69   Memo from Lord Schuster, Permanent Secretary of the Lord Chancellor's Office, 1943 – cited in R. Stevens, *The Independence of the Judiciary*, p.3.
70   See p. 45.
71   See p.129ff.

venerable age. Broadly speaking, there are two 'tradition' arguments. The first is represented by the adage: 'if it ain't broke, don't fix it'. The Lord Chancellor's judicial functions are defended by insistences that *"we wouldn't start from here, but it works"*[72] and *"we live by what is reasonable, not by what is rational."*[73] Such comments are inaccurate: the problems outlined above demonstrate quite clearly that the current system does *not* work satisfactorily.

The second argument is that, as a symbolic bulwark of the British constitution for so long, overwhelming reform to the office of Lord Chancellor would be an inherently undesirable inroad into the nation's political heritage. This is a very weak point. Just as it is wrong to criticise a harmless tradition purely because it is old,[74] it is wrong to defend damaging customs simply on the basis of their longevity. The public interest arguments against the Lord Chancellor being head of the judiciary and sitting as a judge are strong, based as they are upon judicial independence, the rule of law and public confidence in the judiciary. It will take more than the 'age card' to even the scales.

In fact, the Lord Chancellor's role as head of the judiciary (as we now know it) was only first recognised in the eighteenth century.[75] The Lord Chancellor had no judicial role at all until the fourteenth century,[76] three centuries after the starting point preferred by most constitutional historians for the office itself[77] and seven hundred years after the beginning postulated by others.[78] The functions of the post have

---

72   See Andrew Tyrie MP, *The Chancellor's Department: Time to Go* (December 2002, unpublished).

73   Edward Garnier QC MP, *Good Riddance? The Office of the Lord Chancellor: What is the Government Up To, and Do We Care?, Counsel*, July 2003.

74   On which see our conclusions as to retaining the title of Lord Chancellor for the Speaker of the House of Lords – see pp.110–112.

75   Lord Hailsham, *A Sparrow's Flight* (Collins, 1990) p.379.

76   Underhill, *The Lord Chancellor*, (Terence Dalton, 1978), p.75.

77   See Underhill, *The Lord Chancellor* (Terence Dalton, 1978) p.1; Sir William Anson, *The Law and Custom of the Constitution*, Vol II, Part 1 (4th edn, Clarendon Press, 1935).

78   The first holder of the office was Andgmendus in 605AD, according to the old LCD website and Lord MacKay, *The Lord Chancellor in the 1990s* (1991) 44 *Current Legal Problems* 241.

evolved very flexibly over time.[79] Therefore, if – as we later advocate[80] – the office of Lord Chancellor were to survive in a truncated, non-judicial form, it cannot be said that it has lost one of its inherent features.

The Lord Chancellor's Ministerial Responsibilities

Abolishing the Lord Chancellor's Department

Having opted to reallocate the Lord Chancellor's functions as head of the judiciary and to terminate his right to sit as a judge, the Government has also transferred his ministerial responsibilities to the Department for Constitutional Affairs, to be headed by a 'conventional' minister.

The Lord Chancellor's Department was responsible for a wide range of issues, many of fundamental importance to the individual and/or the state. They include: the administration of justice; legal aid; civil law reform; devolution issues; human rights; electoral law and party funding; constitutional reform; referenda; freedom of information; royal, Church and hereditary issues; family justice, including marriage, divorce and relationship support. Moreover, as a recent paper published by the Institute for Public Policy Research demonstrates, the LCD received an annual budget of some £2.5 billion.[81]

As Andrew Tyrie MP emphasised to us, control of such a large budget and such contentious matters should not be reserved for an unelected peer who is not directly accountable in the Chamber of the House of Commons, but only in the less taxing and lower profile atmosphere of the Lords.[82] Sir Nicholas Lyell QC rightly observed that

---

79   See Woodhouse, *The Office of Lord Chancellor*, (Hart Publishing, 2001), Introduction.
80   See pp.110–112.
81   Spencer, *Time for a Ministry of Justice?* (Institute for Public Policy Research, 2001), p.10; the point is also made in Woodhouse, *The Office of Lord Chancellor*, (Hart Publishing, 2001), p.12.
82   The junior ministers in his department may include MPs, but without the head of department in the Commons, his policies enjoy a lower profile in the elected House and their principal author is unable to support them and be held accountable for them in front of MPs.

it should not be ruled out altogether that, in certain circumstances, a Lord might head the department.[83] But this should be the exception, not the norm; if these responsibilities remained with the Lord Chancellor, they could *only ever* be controlled by a member of the House of Lords. Therefore, the Government's conversion of the Lord Chancellor's Department into the Department for Constitutional Affairs – headed by a minister who in future will not be Lord Chancellor – is to be welcomed, although it is regrettable that the very first such minister is himself an unelected peer.

It has also been said that the Lord Chancellor's position as a member of the government is incompatible with his role as speaker of the House of Lords:

> *"The role is effectively that of impartial chair, in debates that frequently focus on government business. As such, the position ought not to be filled by a member of the government, however well he might fulfil it in practice."* [84]

Particular concern was expressed in 2001 at the fact that, when asserting in a debate that *"it is not the case that the Lord Chancellor is not party political,"* Lord Irvine *"answered his critics in the House standing feet from the Woolsack from which at other times he exercises his neutral role as chair."*[85]

It is certainly axiomatic that the Speaker of the House of Commons, whilst originating from a party-political background as an MP, should be neutral at all times; hence the controversy in 2001 over allegations that Michael Martin retained a political agenda.[86] On the other hand, the Lord

---

83 *"Just as I wouldn't rule it out that the Foreign Secretary would be a Lord, like Lord Carrington, a very distinguished Foreign Secretary apart from the Falklands."*

84 Spencer, *Time for a Ministry of Justice?* (Institute for Public Policy Research, 2001), p.11.

85 *ibid.*

86 See *Speaker Close to Apology Over Asylum Remarks*, The Daily Telegraph, 31st October 2001.

Chancellor's influence as Speaker is much more limited than that of his Commons counterpart. In particular, he does not call upon members to speak and has no powers to call the House to order; the House regulates itself. However, if the House of Lords is properly to be modernised, the position of Speaker may well have to be strengthened. This would accordingly be a further reason for transferring the Lord Chancellor's ministerial responsibilities to a department headed by a 'conventional' minister.

Time for a 'Ministry of Justice'?

> "One of the worst features of these proposals is that Mr Blunkett has won a famous victory in blocking what needed to be done, which was to create a single department responsible for both civil and criminal law. One goes on having this inefficient divide between the Home Office and what was the Lord Chancellor's Department, which I thought was very bad when I worked at the Home Office from 1974 to 1976, and nothing's happened since that's altered my view about that." – Lord Lester of Herne Hill QC

The term 'Ministry of Justice' conjures up different images for different people. Lord Haldane in 1918 saw such a ministry as the product of amalgamating the Lord Chancellor's Department and the Home Office.[87] Others have used the term to describe what has now ended up as the Department for Constitutional Affairs: no more and no less than a translation of the LCD.[88] The third model, which is what most commentators now mean when they refer to a 'Ministry of Justice', would be the result of some form of realignment between the roles of the LCD and the Home Office.[89] During the course of our interviews, we have learnt that the possibility for a Ministry of Justice along the lines of this third model,

---

87   See Woodhouse, *The Office of Lord Chancellor*, (Hart Publishing, 2001), p.208.
88   Woodhouse, *The Office of Lord Chancellor*, (Hart Publishing, 2001), p.210.
89   See *Reform of the Lord Chancellor's Department* (JUSTICE Briefing Paper, June 2003), paragraphs 5 and 26; Spencer, *Time for a Ministry of Justice?* (Institute for Public Policy Research, 2001), *in passim*.

to be headed by an MP, was seriously considered in early June. However, when Number 10 tested the water by leaking the proposal to newspapers a few days before the reforms were announced, violent opposition from David Blunkett to the carving out of powers from his Home Office fiefdom was enough to scupper the plans.[90]

The principal responsibility which advocates of a Ministry of Justice would like to see added to the LCD's existing powers under the new department is criminal law reform. This is currently controlled by the Home Office, under the heading 'Criminal Justice', which also includes criminal policy, prisons, probation and drugs.[91] Criminal procedure – including the criminal courts and legal aid – and *civil* law reform are already controlled by the LCD / DCA.

The objections to the Home Office's ongoing control of criminal law reform are twofold. Firstly, the argument goes, a Home Secretary's criminal justice priority is law enforcement. This is an operational function, and has key relevance to matters such as policing strategy, the probation service and prisons. However, law reform – a discipline which is structural, not operational – and law enforcement are two distinct matters; the former should not be dictated by the latter.

> "The criminal law should not simply be used as a tool of law enforcement but to protect the innocent. It serves no-ones' interests if the guilty go free and the innocent are convicted. The principles of justice would be better served if the criminal law were the responsibility of... a department grounded in principles of justice, fairness and proportionality – not a department judged on the extent to which it is seen to be tough on offenders" – **Institute for Public Policy Research**[92]

---

90   See also George Jones, *Irvine 'to Go in Summer Reshuffle'*, *Daily Telegraph*, 5th June 2003; Patrick Wintour and Nicholas Wyatt, *Blunkett Fights Off Ministry of Justice Plan*, *The Guardian*, 12th June 2003.

91   See *List of Ministerial Responsibilities*, Cabinet Office, October 2002; Spencer, *Time for a Ministry of Justice?* (Institute for Public Policy Research, 2001), p.3.

92   Spencer, *Time for a Ministry of Justice?* (Institute for Public Policy Research, 2001).

The most frequently cited example of this problem is the codification of the criminal law, which is currently scattered amongst manifold statutes and endless case law. There is a general, non party-political consensus that codification is a necessary and long overdue reform, in order to clarify to individuals the limits of permissible conduct.[93] The Law Commission has done the drafting, at public expense;[94] all that needs doing is to enshrine it in statute. *"The Home Office, however, has no interest – precisely because its focus is operational and not strategic. Its emphasis is on crime reduction not crime definition."*[95]

Secondly, it is said that the spread of responsibility for criminal law and procedure, between which there is considerable practical overlap, over two departments with different personnel and different priorities is inefficient:

> *"It results in considerable delay in securing agreement on policy and on budgets, with decisions on which no agreement can be reached hanging between the departments unresolved….The need to secure agreement… absorbs excessive time from officials and is the cause of much frustration."*[96]

There is also a case for switching other functions from the Home Office to the LCD's replacement. Since the Home Office oversees the police in England and Wales, it would seem advisable to transfer its responsibility for the authority dealing with complaints against the police, in order to secure its independence under Article 6(1) ECHR.[97] We agree with JUSTICE's suggestion that the Government's proposed Single

---

93   See Glazebrook, *Still No Code!* in Dockray (ed.), *City University Centenary Lectures in Law* (Blackstone Press, 1996), p.1.

94   On which see the succinct account of Padfield, *Criminal Law*, (3rd edn., Butterworths, 2002), p.18.

95   *Reform of the Lord Chancellor's Department* (JUSTICE Briefing Paper, June 2003), paragraph 28.

96   Spencer, *Time for a Ministry of Justice?* (Institute for Public Policy Research, 2001), p.8 – citing the delay in securing agreement on juvenile justice reforms as one such example.

97   See *Reform of the Lord Chancellor's Department* (JUSTICE Briefing Paper, June 2003), paragraph 30; Spencer, *Time for a Ministry of Justice?* (Institute for Public Policy Research, 2001), p.15.

Equality Body, which would replace the three existing anti-discrimination commissions (currently the responsibility of three different Government departments), ought to fall under the responsibility of the Department for Constitutional Affairs.[98] There are strong objections to the likely alternative, the Home Office, retaining responsibility for policy on race and religion:

> *"Race equality sits uncomfortably with* [the Home Office's] *responsibility for immigration control, policy on the latter long blamed for souring public attitudes towards minorities rather than, as once hoped, improving relations by reassuring the white majority."*[99]

In light of these problems with the current distribution of responsibilities, it is regrettable that an individual politician's ego has prevailed over the public interest benefits which the creation of a fully-blown Ministry of Justice would have achieved.

Other outstanding questions as to the distribution of certain particular functions of the Lord Chancellor, such as his ecclesiastical patronage and visitatorial role,[100] relate to specialist topics outside our remit and shall not be discussed in this book.

Qualifications of the new Minister

There is no formal requirement that the Lord Chancellor should have a professional qualification in English Law.[101] In practice, however, the last non-lawyer to hold the position was Lord Shaftesbury, who resigned in

---

98   *Reform of the Lord Chancellor's Department* (JUSTICE Briefing Paper, June 2003), paragraph 31.

99   Spencer, *Time for a Ministry of Justice?* (Institute for Public Policy Research, 2001), p.5.

100   See *Constitutional Reform: Reforming the Office of the Lord Chancellor* (Department for Constitutional Affairs), p.23ff.

101   See Heuston, *Lives of the Lord Chancellors 1940-1940* (Clarendon Press, 1964), p.4. The lack of stipulations as to professional qualification *"was demonstrated by the appointment in 1987 of Lord Mackay, who came from a Scottish law background"* [Woodhouse, *The Office of Lord Chancellor* (Hart Publishing, 2001) p.9].

1673.[102] Although, unlike the Lord Chancellor, the new Secretary of State for Constitutional Affairs will not hear legal cases as a judge, the number of 'legal-related' issues for which he will have responsibility might indicate that it would be desirable for a convention to arise that he should be legally qualified. However, all the interviewees whom we asked expressed the contrary view. On balance, we agree. As Paul Stinchcombe MP explained, most policy areas that have legal implications, such as constitutional reform, remain predominantly political issues, which a non-legally trained minister could easily control – just as the Secretary of State for Health does not need to be a doctor in order to understand the policy areas covered by his department.

A 'Rump' Lord Chancellor

Whilst we have concluded that the Lord Chancellor should cease sitting as a judge, being head of the judiciary and leading an important ministerial department, none of the arguments used thus far raise any objection to the title continuing to be used for future Speakers of the House of Lords – who would be independent from the executive and chosen by the House itself.

Under this model, the Lord Chancellor would, as now, sit on the Woolsack during debates and carry out ceremonial duties at events such as the State Opening of Parliament. The argument in favour is based purely on tradition: once its objectionable aspects are removed, why abolish altogether an institution that is older than Parliament itself and a cornerstone of our political heritage?

> "The Lord Chancellor has been around for 1,400 years, and it reminds us we have a continuous history going back 1,400 years. How many countries can say that?" – **Michael Beloff QC**

---

102   Lord Kilmuir, Office of the Lord Chancellor (1956) 9 Parliamentary Affairs 132, at p.133.

The Government's initial announcement of its judicial reforms appeared to leave no scope for such a move: we were told that the post of Lord Chancellor was to be abolished altogether. Later in June 2003, it appeared that a retreat might be on the cards. In an interview with *The Daily Telegraph*, Lord Williams of Mostyn, the Leader of the House of Lords until his recent untimely death, said that the idea of preserving the title for the Speaker of the House *"had been put to him by many peers"* and would seriously be considered by the Government.[103]

It was therefore surprising to see that, in September 2003, the Department for Constitutional Affairs' 'consultation' paper on the office of Lord Chancellor dismissed this possibility out of hand – without asking for consultation on the issue, and devoting just forty-four words to explaining its reasons:

> *"Part of the purpose of reforming the office of Lord Chancellor is to address the confusion of roles his office has produced. To create a new office (or rename an existing one) will in all probability add to that confusion, rather than reduce it."*[104]

Leaving aside the unprecedented use of a mere three lines to justify the curtailment of a thousand years of tradition – on an issue that should ultimately be for the House of Lords itself to decide – this argument does not stand up to close examination. The public would not be confused. The Lord Chancellor's greatly truncated role as Speaker and no more would be made perfectly clear through the huge media coverage of the Government's judicial reforms, the renaming of the Lord Chancellor's Department, the public profile of the new

---

103 Rachel Sylvester and Joshua Rozenberg, Title of Lord Chancellor May be Saved in Shake-Up, The Daily Telegraph, 20th June 2003.

104 *Constitutional Reform: Reforming the Office of Lord Chancellor* (Department for Constitutional Affairs, September 2003), p.15.

head of the judiciary and the future absence of the Lord Chancellor as a judge.

Paul Stinchcombe MP raised a separate objection to keeping the Lord Chancellor as Speaker: that the very office – with its antiquated attire, famously mocked by Tony Blair[105] – was a matter of general ridicule, which undermined public confidence in the political system. However, we are not convinced that this captures the public mood. The speaker of the House of Commons wears a similarly unusual outfit, for which he is not mocked. Even if the argument is well grounded, it is not decisive: if his dress really was a problem, the Lord Chancellor could simply wear a business suit.

Accordingly, we strongly oppose the Government's apparent disinclination even to allow the House of Lords to vote upon whether its speaker should continue to be called Lord Chancellor. The brevity and weakness of its sole argument in favour of the complete abolition of this ancient political heritage suggest that the real reason is either a fear that a retreat from the June 12th announcements would prove too embarrassing, or an inherent distaste for all tradition.

The New Head of the Judiciary

Launching the Government's consultation papers on judicial reform, Lord Falconer said in July 2003:

> *"The Secretary of State for Constitutional Affairs will remain, after the abolition of the post of Lord Chancellor, responsible for ensuring the independence of the judiciary in England and Wales within Cabinet and consideration should be given to whether that responsibility should be embedded in legislation."*[106]

---

105   H.C. Debs, col. 363, 18th June 2003.
106   H.L. Debs, col. 632, 14th July 2003. See p.101.

In some quarters, this rather ambiguous statement, repeated almost verbatim in an interview with *The Times* in September, has been interpreted as meaning that *"Falconer insists that he will still act as head of the judiciary."*[107] If it were true, this would be a frightening development: all the problems discussed above with regard to the Lord Chancellor's position as head of the judiciary would be amplified, since the Secretary of State for Constitutional Affairs would be an even more 'political' minister and far less senior than the Lord Chancellor.

However, this does not seem a likely scenario. The Government's consultation paper on judicial appointments talks of the Lord Chief Justice as the *"effective replacement for the Lord Chancellor as Head of the Judiciary of England and Wales."*[108] The paper suggests that complaints against and discipline of judges – traditionally part of the Lord Chancellor's role as head of the judiciary – should be transferred from the executive either to the Lord Chief Justice or to an independent body.[109] In late September, we asked the Department for Constitutional Affairs for clarification; we were assured that the head of the judiciary will indeed be a judge and that the Secretary of State for Constitutional Affairs would simply be responsible for defending judicial independence in Cabinet meetings.[110]

There is near unanimity that *"the most logical arrangement for England and Wales would be that the role of head of the judiciary is taken up by the Lord Chief Justice."*[111] The holder of this office is already the most senior judge in England and Wales, and the title 'Chief Justice' has strong connotations of hierarchical supremacy.[112] This does leave two

---

107 Frances Gibb, *Closing the Silk Route is not a 'Done Deal'*, *The Times*, 23rd September 2003.
108 *Constitutional Reform: A New Way of Appointing Judges* (Department for Constitutional Affairs, July 2003), p.49.
109 *ibid.*, p.50.
110 See pp.100–101
111 *Reform of the Lord Chancellor's Department* (JUSTICE Briefing Paper, June 2003), paragraph 34.
112 In a plethora of nations throughout the world (of which there are too many to mention!) the head of the judiciary bears the title 'Chief Justice'.

further questions to be resolved. Should the position of Lord Chief Justice incorporate the former office of Senior Law Lord, so that one judge is both head of the judiciary and President of the Supreme Court? There are two objections to such a move. Firstly, as Roger Smith observed to us, the two roles require somewhat different capabilities. The position of head of the judiciary is largely a figurehead, whilst the primary functions of the President of the Supreme Court are administrative.[113] Secondly, combining the functions of both jobs with the everyday duty to hear appeals and deliver judgments might be too much for one individual. It would therefore seem better to retain both the President of the Supreme Court and the Lord Chief Justice as separate offices.

The next question is whether, as head of the judiciary, the Lord Chief Justice should be a member of the Supreme Court. Under the current system, the Lord Chief Justice usually sits in the Court of Appeal but, as a holder of 'high judicial office' who is also a member of the House of Lords, he is eligible to sit on the Appellate Committee. However, this criterion for *ex officio* membership is to end upon the Supreme Court's creation – and we have recommended that the practice of retaining a part-time reserve list for the highest court should be abolished altogether.[114] The Lord Chief Justice would accordingly be either in or out. On balance, it would seem preferable for him to remain in the Court of Appeal. If he were to be member of the Supreme Court, despite being the head of the judiciary in England and Wales, he would give the appearance of playing second fiddle to the President of the Supreme Court. However, if he remained in the Court of Appeal, he could continue to be President of its Criminal Division and of the Queens Bench Division of the High Court – roles befitting the head of the

---

113 See pp. 75–77
114 See pp.68–70

judiciary. His absence from the highest court would not, in all probability, detract from his public standing; Lord Woolf already has a very high profile and commands great respect from the media, despite being based in the Court of Appeal.

4. Judicial Appointments

Who Should Appoint Judges?

Ending the Government's input

Currently, law lords, Court of Appeal judges and Heads of Division in the High Court are appointed by the Queen on the recommendation of the Prime Minister, who in turn is presented with an informal shortlist by the Lord Chancellor.[1] The usual extent of the Prime Minister's input is not clear; however, there is firsthand evidence that Margaret Thatcher took a proactive role in selection[2] and that John Major did not always accept the preferred candidate of his Lord Chancellor, Lord Mackay.[3] If it is indeed Prime Ministerial practice to 'interfere' in senior judicial appointments in this way, this would seem to be a substantial infringement of judicial independence.[4] But even if Prime Ministers are

---

1   The Queen's role, which is entirely passive, exists because judges are Crown appointments.
2   By Lord Hailsham's own account – see Lewis, *Lord Hailsham: A Life* (Pimlico, 1998); Woodhouse, *The Office of Lord Chancellor* (Hart Publishing, 2001), pp.133-134.
3   As indicated by Lord Mackay in his evidence to the Home Affairs Committee in 1996 [*Judicial Appointments Procedures* (1995-96) H.C. 52-II, Q.459].
4   Discussed in detail in Chapters One and Three.

generally passive, their continued role serves to undermine public confidence in the judiciary as free from the Government's influence. To quote Sir Thomas Legg, former permanent secretary to the Lord Chancellor's Department:

> *"The Prime Minister's inevitable high party political profile could fuel suspicions, however unjust, of a party or governmental slant to appointments."* [5]

As argued in Chapter One, public confidence in the judiciary depends upon public perceptions of it. Accordingly, the Prime Minister's role in appointing senior judges should be terminated, as was recommended by the Home Affairs Committee in 1996.[6]

All other full-time judges in England and Wales are appointed by the Queen on the direct recommendation of the Lord Chancellor, assisted by around 140 civil servants. Logically extended, Sir Thomas' objection also applies to this system as well. Like the Prime Minister, the Lord Chancellor has a *"high party political profile"* – one which has steadily become more prominent over the past half century.[7] This problem was highlighted in 2001 when Lord Irvine *"faced calls for his resignation… after he admitted asking lawyers who depend on him for their promotions to give money to the Labour Party"* at fundraising dinners and in personal letters. His addressees included those who were likely candidates for judicial appointments.[8] Lord Irvine's unapologetic response was: *"it is not the case that the Lord Chancellor is not party political"* – which hardly dispelled any perceptions of 'political favouritism' in the appoint-

---

5   Sir Thomas Legg, *Judges for the New Century* (2001) P.L. 74, at p.74.
6   But never implemented. See *Judicial Appointments Procedures* (1995-96) H.C. 52-II.
7   See p.88ff.
8   Benedict Brogan, *Irvine in Funds for Jobs Row*, The Daily Telegraph, 19th February 2001.

ments process.[9] If the Lord Chancellor's roles as a judge and as head of the judiciary are to be terminated – as we recommend[10] – this predicament would become even more apparent: he would now be a purely 'political' figure. We therefore welcome the Government's proposal to remove this further responsibility from the Lord Chancellor.

The two primary alternatives to the Lord Chancellor's unfettered initiative in judicial appointments are the election of judges or the establishment of an independent Judicial Appointments Commission. The first of these options has been rightly dismissed. The example in the United States demonstrates that it would lead to the politicisation of the judiciary, with judges selected on the basis of their social or political affiliations rather than on merit.[11]

Proponents of the existing discretion of the Lord Chancellor argue that a Judicial Appointments Commission would itself politicise the judiciary. However, this need not be the case. As we explain later, much depends upon the composition of the commission and the criteria for appointment.[12] It has also been suggested that, in contrast to the Lord Chancellor, a Commission might tend to make 'safe' decisions, preferring to appoint judges on the basis of seniority rather than any particular flair.[13] However, there is no empirical evidence to support this: as Dr Kate Malleson insisted, a less experienced but manifestly exceptionally talented candidate would surely be recognised no less by an independent commission than by a Cabinet minister.

---

9   *ibid.*
10   See Chapter Three, *passim.*
11   See *Constitutional Reform: A New Way of Appointing Judges* (Department for Constitutional Affairs, July 2003) p.75.
12   See pp.124–125
13   See *Reform of the Lord Chancellor's Department* (JUSTICE Briefing Paper, June 2003), paragraph 14.

An independent commission – to appoint or to recommend?

There are three principal alternatives for the extent to which a Judicial Appointments Commission could control appointments to the Bench:

- Actual *selection* of the successful candidate for any given judicial position, directly advising the Queen without any ministerial involvement

- *Nomination* of a single candidate for any given judicial position. Advising the Queen would be left to the relevant minister, who would be able to veto the nomination.

- *Presenting a shortlist* of candidates for any given judicial position to the minister, who would be at liberty to advise the Queen to appoint any one of them.

Whilst opening the issue up for consultation, the Government has expressed its disinclination to implement the first of these models, an appointing commission with no ministerial involvement.[14] The advantage of such a model is that it is the purest in terms of independence: it would minimalise the prospects of any particular appointment appearing to be made according to executive or party-political interests.[15] However, the Government's consultation paper rightly observes that, since judges are appointed by the Crown, the lack of ministerial involvement in recommending candidates to the Queen would run against a fundamental tenet of British constitutional democracy:

> *"One of the limitations on the power of the Crown, in our constitutional monarchy, is that the Queen acts formally on the advice of Her Ministers, who are accountable to Parliament. As one*

---

14   *Constitutional Reform: A New Way of Appointing Judges* (Department for Constitutional Affairs, July 2003) pp.24-26.

15   Although the means by which members of the Commission are to be selected could leave some scope for controversy – see pp.124–125.

aspect of this principle, it is constitutional practice that The Sovereign, when making appointments, does so only on the advice of Ministers. This ensures that Ministers and not the Crown personally can be held accountable to Parliament for the appointments process."[16]

All of our interviewees questioned on this point agreed that some level of ministerial accountability was necessary. As Dr Kate Malleson said, *"there needs to be a link to the democratic system."*

However, to allow the minister to choose from the Commission's 'shortlist' – the option favoured by the Government[17] – would have all the same problems as full appointment by the Lord Chancellor. In fact the potential for public perception that judicial appointments are motivated by 'political' factors may be greater. The minister involved will no longer be the head of the judiciary or a judge himself, and so his executive and party political guises will be even more at the forefront than before.

Therefore, we advocate the second model: 'nomination with veto'. Whilst the identity of a vetoed candidate ought not to be made public without his permission, for fear of damaging his credibility, it should be the minister's statutory duty immediately to declare any exercise of the veto.[18] This scrutiny would hopefully prevent unnecessary ministerial interference with the Commission's choices and should in practice result in the convention that the veto is exercised only *in extremis*; normally, the word of the Commission would be final and the minister

---

16   *Constitutional Reform: A New Way of Appointing Judges* (Department for Constitutional Affairs, July 2003), p.24.

17   *Constitutional Reform: A Supreme Court for the United Kingdom* (Department for Constitutional Affairs, July 2003), p.30.

18   A more effective scrutiny than the Government's suggestion that statistics on the use of the veto should be made available in the Commission's annual report – *Constitutional Reform: A New Way of Appointing Judges* (Department for Constitutional Affairs, July 2003), p. 26.

would simply act as a conduit for recommending appointments to the Queen.[19]

It has been suggested in some quarters that, whilst Lord Chancellor should lose his roles as judge, head of the judiciary and head of a high spending government department, the office should survive the present reforms as a ministry for judicial appointments.[20] However, that model supposes that judicial appointments should remain largely in the hands of the Lord Chancellor. Since we recommend that the Government's role should be limited to a veto, we do not see the need for a separate ministry and propose that this veto should rest in the Secretary of State for Constitutional Affairs. In our view, the title of Lord Chancellor would most appropriately be continued by being conferred upon the Speaker of the House of Lords, who would be independent of the executive and would have no judicial role at all.[21]

Selection of judges for the Supreme Court

The Department for Constitutional Affairs' consultation paper on judicial appointments rightly observes that it would be inappropriate for judges of the Supreme Court, a court of the whole United Kingdom, to be recommended by the Judicial Appointments Commission for England and Wales.[22] It suggests two alternatives. Firstly, it moots the idea of the Prime Minister continuing to advise the Queen on the appointment of judges for the highest court, but on the advice of the First Minister in Scotland and the First and Deputy First Ministers in

---

19   And virtually always the case with lower judicial appointments, which even under the current system are merely 'rubber-stamped' by the Lord Chancellor upon the recommendation of his civil servants, due to the vast bulk of applications [In 2001/2002, 4,225 applications for judicial appointments resulted in 915 applications – 140 civil servants processed them – see *Constitutional Reform: A New Way of Appointing Judges* (Department for Constitutional Affairs, July 2003) p. 12].
20   Lord Alexander of Weedon, H.L. Debs., col. 116, 8 September 2003.
21   See pp.110–112.
22   *Constitutional Reform: A Supreme Court for the United Kingdom* (Department for Constitutional Affairs, July 2003) pp.28-31.

Northern Ireland. The second proposed option would be for the Prime Minster to consult the heads of the devolved governments after receiving a shortlist from the Judicial Appointments Commission.

These proposals threaten both actual and perceived judicial independence even more than the present arrangements. Both models leave appointment of the country's top judges to the ultimate discretion of the most party-political minister of them all, who need not have legal qualifications and – where he was previously advised by the Lord Chancellor, who was head of the judiciary – would be advised by two other 'pure politicians'. Such an approach completely contradicts and heavily undermines the underlying principle of the proposed reforms to the judicial infrastructure – securing judges' independence from politics and politicians in the eyes of the public.

A preferable alternative would be for the Scottish and Northern Irish members of the Supreme Court to be appointed by the domestic judicial appointments commissions already operating in those countries.[23] The Government has refused to consult on this option on the ground that *"the Court will sit as a single UK court and it is important that it is seen to be a collegiate body."*[24] However, we consider that any inroad into perceptions of the Court as a collegiate body under this model would be less acute and would have less grave implications than the threats to the Court's perceived and actual independence under the systems favoured by the Government.

Composition of the Judicial Appointments Commission

Membership

The Government's consultation paper has proposed that one third of

23   The current convention is that there are two Scottish and one Northern Irish members of the Appellate Committee. See p. 22.

24   *Constitutional Reform: A Supreme Court for the United Kingdom* (Department for Constitutional Affairs, July 2003), p.28.

the Judicial Appointments Commission should be 'lay' people – in other words, individuals from a background outside law – *"who should as far as possible be reflective of the community."*[25]

The case for including lay people upon the Commission is that they will add a different perspective to that of judges and lawyers and accordingly prevent what Andrew Tyrie MP called *"a self-perpetuating oligarchy in the profession."* As Dr Kate Malleson and Robin Allen QC emphasised to us, the function of judges does not simply depend upon legal expertise, but increasingly involves the exercise of 'value judgments' – largely thanks to our common law system (whereby judges can 'make' law themselves), the increasing remit of judicial review and the incorporation of the European Convention on Human Rights.[26] Therefore, the argument goes, the appointment of the judges who are going to make those important value judgements should not be monopolised by one profession, in which certain values may be disproportionately predominant as compared to society at large. A more general advantage of lay people having a role in selecting judges is that it would facilitate greater diversity at the bench, since existing judges and lawyers would tend *"to appoint in their own image and kind."*[27] Thirdly, from a presentational perspective, for judicial appointments to be left solely to the legal profession would do little to counter the popular image of the judiciary as inaccessible and lacking openness.[28]

Whilst these arguments have some force, a far greater concern in our view is the danger that the inclusion of lay people would politicise the whole process and compromise judicial independence. Judges and lawyers would enter into the judicial appointments process from a professional angle: any latent political sympathies they might have would

---

25   *Constitutional Reform: A New Way of Appointing Judges* (Department for Constitutional Affairs, July 2003) p. 56.
26   See p.130ff.
27   JUSTICE, evidence to the Home Affairs Committee, 1996.
28   For the predominance of these criticisms, See pp.40–41 and Genn, *Paths to Justice: What People Do and Think about Going to Law* (Hart Publishing, 1999) pp.239-247.

be uninfluential. Conversely, in the absence of any legal expertise, lay people on the Commission would inevitably have their political values and agendaat the forefront of their minds. Moreover, since there is no alternative but for lay members of the Commission to be appointed – directly or, via a 'recommending body' of the kind proposed in the consultation paper,[29] indirectly – by the Department for Constitutional Affairs, it is very likely that the individuals selected for the role would often be 'political animals' sympathetic to the Government of the day. Most tellingly, statistics from 2000 indicate that 67% of 'quango' members in the UK in that year had a declared affiliation with the Labour Party – a grossly disproportionate number by any standard.[30] Needless to say, any such party-political influence and indirect executive control (which, unlike the Lord Chancellor, would undoubtedly often be *actual* and not just perceived) over the appointment of judges would grossly undermine the independence of the judiciary and the rule of law. These fundamental values must take precedence over the admittedly strong arguments in favour of including lay people; the Commission should consist solely of lawyers and judges. Besides, the need for a diverse judiciary and the issue of the judiciary's public image can be addressed in other ways than by having lay members on the Commission.[31]

> "I am hugely sceptical of the capacity of lay people to set themselves a non-partisan agenda." – **Professor Ian Loveland**

Some of our consultees thought that at least one place on the Commission should be reserved for a legal academic. However, whilst we would certainly welcome the lifting of current restrictions on

---

29 See pp.126–127.
30 See, for example, *Quango: Spelt SQA or STB?, The Scots Independent,* 17th November 2000.
31 See pp. 135. Hopefully, public perceptions of the judiciary will improve as a result of the wider reform programme – in particular, the creation of a Supreme Court and the end of the executive's (at the very least perceived) influence of the judiciary through the position of the Lord Chancellor.

academics sitting as judges in the Court of Appeal and above,[32] we are unconvinced as to the appropriateness of their presence on the Commission. As Professor Loveland observed, the nature of academics' work and their absence from the courts means that they generally do not have any 'insider' experience of what it takes to be a good judge, especially in the High Court and below, where cases are often decided by resolving factual disputes rather than points of law.

Size of the Commission

The Government has proposed that the Commission should have fifteen members: five lawyers, five judges and five non-lawyers.[33] This size has drawn criticism from Roger Smith and Robert Marshall-Andrews QC MP, who pointed to the trend of such large committees to split and factionalise. This seems to be a forceful argument, and so we see no need to 'replace' the lay element having decided to exclude it. Nine members would be favourable to ten, so as to avoid a tie. As the new head of the judiciary, the Lord Chief Justice should chair the Commission.[34]

Selection of members

> "I would have thought that, once established, this Commission should be self sufficient and not require government agency to direct its membership thereafter." – **Lord Justice Laws**

The Department for Constitutional Affairs' consultation paper proposes that members of the Judicial Appointments Commission will themselves be selected by a Government-appointed 'recommending

---

32   See pp. 70–71
33   *Constitutional Reform: A New Way of Appointing Judges* (Department for Constitutional Affairs, July 2003) pp. 55-57.
34   His inclusion on the Commission is discussed at p. 128.

body' of four, which would be chaired by the Permanent Secretary of the Department for Constitutional Affairs.[35] We strongly oppose this model: the benefits of curtailing the Minister's involvement in the selection of judges would be severely limited if the Commission members who were to replace him in this role were handpicked by his right-hand man in the civil service and three of his own appointees. Besides, the idea of establishing an appointing committee at public expense purely to appoint another appointing committee seems nothing short of farcical.

> "Government appointing the appointments committee to appoint the commission to appoint judges – talk about smoke and mirrors!" – Sir Nicholas Lyell QC

The alternative mooted in the Government's consultation paper is that some committee members should be nominated from their respective professional bodies: namely, the Judges Council, the Bar Council and the Law Society.[36]

With regard to the judicial members of the Commission, this would seem inadvisable. 'Political machinations' such as lobbying for the Judges' Council's nomination are as inappropriate for judges as overt party-political activities are. Notably, in Italy, the election of judges by their peers to sit on a judicial appointments committee has led to a stark politicisation of the judiciary.[37]

> "My preference would be to have as few people as possible appointed to the appointments commission by the exercise of discretion." – Dr Christopher Forsyth

---

35   *Constitutional Reform: A New Way of Appointing Judges* (Department for Constitutional Affairs, July 2003) pp 54-55.
36   *Ibid.*, p.59.
37   See Thomas, *Judicial Appointments in Continental Europe*, in *Judicial Appointments Commissions: The European and North American Experience and the Possible Implications for the United Kingdom* (Lord Chancellor's Department, December 1997), p.19ff.

There would be far greater safeguards in having the judicial portion of the commission selected on an *ex officio* basis. We propose that a seat on the Commission should be reserved for each of the 'big five' senior judicial offices: the Lord Chief Justice; the President of the Supreme Court; the Master of the Rolls;[38] the President of the Family Division; the Vice Chancellor.[39] Being already in the public eye as heads of their court or division (and, in the case of the Lord Chief Justice, head of the judiciary under the proposed reforms), these office-holders' presence would provide a greater guarantee of independence and impartiality than any other model for selecting the judicial element of the Commission. Their workload as judges would not be significantly compromised, since usually only senior judicial appointments would require more than merely rubber-stamping the civil servants' recommendations.[40] If any of these office holders was a candidate for promotion (say, to the Supreme Court), he or she would simply stand down from the Commission for the duration of the debate and vote on that appointment.[41]

It makes good sense for the 'lawyer' element of the Commission to be nominated by the Bar Council and Law Society. We propose that there should be two representatives from each; although solicitors will never occupy as many judicial positions as barristers, due to the very nature of their job, they are nonetheless well placed to understand what makes a good judge and add an element of diversity which – in the absence of lay members – a Commission composed solely of barristers and judges would lack. A broader spectrum of perspectives amongst

---

38   The head of the Civil Division of the High Court.

39   The head of the Chancery Division of the High Court. The title 'Vice-Chancellor' might appropriately be changed following the abolition of the Lord Chancellor's judicial roles.

40   As is now the case – see p.122, n. 20.

41   This would be a potential eventuality under any model, unless the judicial selection committee is composed entirely of Supreme Court judges, which would clearly be too narrow an approach. Consideration should be given to whether, in such a situation, the members' vote should be secret.

members of the Commission could also be achieved by stipulating that one of the representatives from each of these unions should be less than thirty-five years old.

> "I would like to see a few younger lawyers on the panel; there's no reason why it shouldn't include them. There is an issue about judges on age; we're not going to have any twenty-eight year old judges, but why not some twenty-eight year olds on the Commission?" – **Dr Kate Malleson**

We therefore recommend that the Judicial Appointments Commission should include the President of the Law Society, the Chairman of the Bar Council and a Judicial Appointments Junior Representative from each body, who would be aged under thirty-five and would be elected on an annual basis by qualified solicitors and barristers who were themselves under thirty-five.

Criteria for Appointing Judges

> "If you ask the average person on the street, the only thing that they can tell you about judges is that they are old and they are men and they are white and they are privately educated, and they are out of touch. Ok, you can say that's just a thumbnail sketch, but if you say that's describing the Court of Appeal and the law lords, it's a pretty accurate sketch. This is undermining the legitimacy of what is in many ways a fabulous bench – intellectually, in its integrity, in its honesty." – **Dr Kate Malleson**

As of 1st April 2002, 85.6% of all judges were male and 14.4% were female. No woman has ever been a member of the Appellate Committee of the House of Lords. There has yet to be an ethnic minority judge in the High Court or above; only 1.2% of circuit judges, 3% of recorders and one deputy High Court judge are ethnic minorities. By way of comparison, the 2001 Census records that 51.3% of those living in England and Wales are women and 8.7% are ethnic minorities.

Such a disproportionate number of white males, many of whom were privately educated, threatens the judiciary's legitimacy amongst other sections of society.[42] If laws are to be respected and obeyed, the public must be able to identify with the judges who interpret, apply and (so far as the common law is concerned) make them. For example, as Roger Smith observed to us:

> "There has to be a sufficient number of black judges in the Crown Courts to give black defendants to be given the sense that they are being judged by a society to which they belong."

The present composition of the judiciary is doubtless a significant reason why 41% of the public consider judges to be 'very out of touch'.[43]

Recognising this problem in its consultation paper on judicial appointments, the Government has expressed its intention to make the judiciary *"more reflective"* of society.[44] Whilst acknowledging that the current composition of the judiciary is far from satisfactory, a number of our consultees were concerned that this aim risked demoting 'merit' as the overriding principle for the selection of judges.

However, in our view, the distinction between 'merit' and 'diversity' is not so clear-cut. As Lord Lester of Herne Hill QC emphasised to us, the definition of 'merit' – so far as judicial appointments are concerned – incorporates more than just technical ability and intellectual brilliance. Particularly in the higher courts, a judge's role has never been confined to the purely black and white task of reaching the 'correct conclusion' as to the interpretation or application of a given legal provision. Under our common law system, judges themselves are law makers; where litigation

---

42   Of the current Lords of Appeal and Lord Justices of Appeal, 86.5% went to public school – see *Backgrounds of the Senior Judiciary* (S. J. Berwin, 2003)

43   *Confidence in the Criminal Justice System: Findings from the British Crime Survey,* Catriona Mirlees-Black, Research Findings No. 137, RDS Home Office. 2000.

44   *Constitutional Reform: A New Way of Appointing Judges* (Department for Constitutional Affairs, July 2003), p.45.

concerns an area on which there is no legislation or binding precedent, they may 'fill the gap', delivering judgments that themselves have precedential force in future cases on the same point. Thus, for example, it is judges who have outlined under what circumstances public authorities may be sued for negligence, who have set out to what extent a defendant's drunkenness should act as mitigation for a criminal offence and who have decided under what circumstances a person should be bound by his promise. In giving these decisions, judges are 'making law', relying not so much upon legal expertise as upon their own value judgments.

As Nicholas Barber observed in our interview, the coming into force of the Human Rights Act 1998 has increased the frequency of cases in which judges are called upon to make value judgments. The most striking example of this is the doctrine of 'proportionality', whereby a human right may permissibly be restricted for public policy reasons, if effect on the right is not disproportionate to the public purpose sought to be achieved.[45] The decision as to whether such an action was disproportionate can only be reached by weighing values against each other. An encyclopaedic knowledge of case law is not enough.

Whilst this in no way necessitates the politicisation or direct electoral accountability of the judiciary, it does mean that a pool of judges selected from a narrow section of society may be found wanting. The composition of the 'judicial class' affects its members: attitudes can be changed or hardened through judges' frequent social and professional interaction. This has a knock-on impact on the quality of decisions: a judiciary more reflective of the demographic composition of society is, collectively, going to be much more understanding of the features of and problems facing certain sections of society than a judiciary composed almost entirely of people from the same background, who – no matter how hard they try – will inevitably find it difficult to empathise.[46]

---

45 See *R v Home Secretary, ex parte Daly* [2001] 2 A.C. 532.
46 Which is why it is not enough that one of the existing criteria for judicial appointments is that a candidate should have an *"understanding of people and society"*.

> "There's a 'closed mindset' problem amongst the judiciary. Addressing that issue requires a system which ensures that you get judges who really understand the nature of society to a sufficient degree to understand and recognize their own prejudices, and put them to one side." – **Robin Allen QC**

So, it is not the case that 'diversity' and 'merit' are two discrete values that run into conflict with each other. Diversity might be more appropriately be called an ingredient of 'merit', since a judiciary with a wider experience of the problems facing society would be more likely to produce judgments capable of meeting those problems. A judiciary more reflective of society, subject to the following important caveats, would enhance, rather than compromise, the overriding principle of meritocracy.

The problem with quotas

> "Quotas would be absolutely disastrous" – **Andrew Tyrie MP**

One move which has been mooted in the context of the present reforms is the imposition of targets or quotas of ethnic minorities and women to be appointed as judges.[47] This would be a disastrous approach, for a number of reasons.

Firstly, quotas or targets would blur the edges between 'diversity' and 'representativeness'. As Sir Sydney Kentridge has recently elucidated, these two concepts are fundamentally different.[48] 'Representative' judges are expected to look out for the interests of those from a similar background to themselves, acting as their 'spokesmen' on the Bench – a frightening prospect for judicial impar-

---

47   See *eg* Clare Dyer, *Falconer Reveals Plans for Judicial Shakeup, The Guardian*, 15th July 2003; *Supreme Court Plans Unveiled*, BBC News Online, 14th July 2003.

48.   Sir Sydney Kentridge, *The Highest Court: Selecting the Judges* (2003) 37 C.L.J. 55, *in passim*.

tiality and the rule of law. Judicial diversity simply requires the pool of judges to be drawn from a wide enough range of backgrounds for the judiciary as a whole to understand the values of contemporary society and to be seen as a legitimate organ by which laws can be made and liberties decided. The latter concept does not require fixed proportions of minorities and women amongst judges; the former does. The aim of quotas or targets would doubtless be for the national breakdown of minorities and women to be replicated amongst the judiciary – such a rigid equivalence would inevitably give the impression that judges *were* the representatives of the sections of society from which they came.

Moreover, quotas or targets would elevate diversity above other vital ingredients of merit, such as legal expertise and technical ability. The most worthy candidates when looked at 'in the round' would not always be selected, in order to make way for less deserving applicants from the 'target sectors'. Such political correctness is not the right way to go about widening the pool of judges. It would also demean those female and ethnic minority barristers who are deservedly appointed to judicial office; their selection would be seen as based solely on their background, undermining their credibility as judges.

In fact, a natural, evolutionary change towards increased diversity is already underway. When most of the present senior judges started their legal careers, opportunities at the Bar were far greater for wealthy, white males. Now, of trainee barristers undertaking pupillage in England and Wales, 47% are women and 20% are from ethnic minorities[49] – over twice the number of ethnic minorities in the country at large.[50] Already, some of the most famous and profitable barristers' chambers in the country are headed by women, the President of the Family Division is

---

49   Bar Council Statistics, 2002.
50   According to the 2001 Census, 8.7% of those living in England and Wales are ethnic minorities.

a woman and there are women judges in the Court of Appeal. There may not yet have been a female judge on the Appellate Committee or an ethnic minority full-time judge in the High Court or above, but there are individuals who appear set to break this record imminently. As Lord Irvine said in 2001:

> *"I would expect to see more women and people from minority ethnic communities being appointed as increasing numbers of practitioners from these groups reach the stage in their professional lives where appointment as a judge becomes a real prospect."*[51]

If such a shift is happening of its own accord, it would seem overly heavy-handed to apply such blunt tools as quotas or targets, with all their ensuing problems.

Pointedly, despite having a recent history overwhelmingly more scarred by social division than our own, South Africa has no set quotas or targets for judicial appointments: its constitution requires simply that the need for the judiciary to broadly reflect the country's racial and gender composition be considered when the selections are made.[52] We would do well to follow suit.

Other ways of encouraging a more diverse judiciary

There are other ways, besides quotas and the presence of lay people on the Judicial Appointments Commission, through which the judiciary can become more reflective of society. This is particularly so, since much of the problem is not that ethnic minorities and women are being discriminated against under the current appointment process, but rather that these groups of people are *"under-represented as a*

---

51   *Annual Report on Judicial Appointments 2001-2001* (Lord Chancellor's Department, 2002), foreword.
52   The Constitution of the Republic of South Africa No. 108 of 1996 section 174(2).

proportion of the total pool of applicants"[53] Potentially meritous candidates are not putting themselves forward for selection. This applies to solicitors as well.[54] Therefore, the focus should in fact be less upon the decision-making process of the Commission and more upon making judicial office attractive to lawyers from all walks of life.

To their credit, the Lord Chancellor's Department, the Bar Council and the Law Society have, in recent years, set up a number of initiatives aimed at casting the net wider. Since 1994, 'judicial appointment roadshow events', have taken place around the country, featuring an LCD presentation followed by audience questions. In 1999, the LCD introduced a 'work shadowing' scheme, with the aim of giving those considering applying for a judicial appointment a direct insight into judges' work; participants follow a Circuit or District Judge for up to five days. In 2001-2, 78 shadowing arrangements were made, of which 56% were solicitors, just under half were female and 6.4% were of ethnic minority origin. The LCD has also co-hosted a session on judicial appointments at the Woman Lawyer Forum and the Minority Lawyer conferences, alongside the Bar Council and the Law Society. It is too early to tell if such initiatives have achieved a sustained, marked increase in the number of applicants for judicial office, but they are undeniably steps in the right direction.

In March 2003, a Bar Council working party chaired by Sir Ian Glidewell, a former Court of Appeal judge, recommended that further initiatives should be adopted – including, for example, an even more extensive programme of workshops and lectures on judicial appointments and *"a mentoring scheme for those seriously interested in pursuing the idea of judicial appointment, particularly those who do not otherwise*

53　Sir Ian Glidewell, *Bar Council Working Party on Judicial Appointments and Silk, Consultation Document* (March 2003), p.34.

54　Even taking into account the fact that many of them – for example those who specialise in non-contentious commercial advisory work – have less relevant experience than barristers and are less suited to judicial office.

have access to appropriate members of the judiciary for advice."[55] Such policies are to be welcomed; the current judicial reforms provide an excellent opportunity for their implementation. In our view, they should be supplemented by a more aggressive approach to marketing judicial 'job opportunities', targeting those sections of the legal profession from which applications have not been forthcoming. For example, advertisements should receive a wider coverage amongst magazines aimed primarily at solicitors and ethnic minority lawyers.[56] The use of professional recruitment consultants to 'headhunt' potentially strong candidates who might otherwise not think of applying should be also given serious consideration.

A further reason for the disproportionately low numbers of female judges and applicants for judicial office is that *"the demands of a judicial post may seem to many women to be irreconcilable with the competing demands of rearing a family."*[57] There are two main reasons for this. Firstly, many judges, from recorders to Lord Justices of Appeal,[58] will have to spend time away from home for prolonged periods. Secondly, in order to progress through the upper echelons of the judicial hierarchy, one needs to hold full-time judicial office for a number of years. For a mother with young children, neither of these may be desirable or even possible. Therefore, in order not to miss out on potentially excellent judges, we recommend that the Judicial Appointments Commission should have the power – under specified circumstances and not before receiving a written application[59] – to impose limitations on a judge's terms of service. In particular, this

---

55   Sir Ian Glidewell, *Bar Council Working Party on Judicial Appointments and Silk, Consultation Document* (March 2003), p.38.
56   Such as *The Lawyer* (a high-circulation magazine catering in particular for solicitors).
57   Sir Ian Glidewell, *Bar Council Working Party on Judicial Appointments and Silk, Consultation Document* (Bar Council, March 2003), p.29.
58   The Court of Appeal is the highest court to go on circuit.
59   The specified circumstances need not necessarily be limited to a judge having to raise a young family – other circumstances could include, for example, the terminal illness of a partner or next of kin.

could include restrictions on the geographical location in which he or she may be required to sit, permitting a permanent High Court judge or Lord Justice of Appeal to sit on a part-time basis, or even (at least at certain levels) allowing a full-scale 'career break' with guarantee of re-entry to the same judicial office upon his or her return.[60]

Such initiatives, coupled with a general requirement that the Judicial Appointments Commission should bear in mind the need for a diverse judiciary when considering applications, should go a long way to increase the legitimacy of the judiciary in the eyes of the public and to ensure that its decisions take greater account of the values of and problems facing contemporary society. Without having to go down the hazardous route of quotas or targets.

A wider pool of judges might also be achieved by establishing a 'career judiciary', recruiting directly from university graduates, as is common in civil law countries such as the Netherlands.[61] However, as all the interviewees whom asked about this concept agreed, our common law legal system is ill-suited to such an approach, being far less 'clinical' and more value laden than the markedly different civil law systems that use a career judiciary.

The Appointments Process: Procedural Aspects

A detailed consideration of the technicalities of Judicial Appointments Commission's everyday practice is best left to specialist publications. However, our consultees did highlight two procedural aspects with important underlying principles, which we shall now turn to.

Firstly, there is an argument that, as our judges take more politically exposed decisions in relation to matters such as human rights, their own

---

60   Subject, of course, to him or her not undertaking any other work in the meantime.
61   Thomas, *Judicial Appointments in Continental Europe*, in *Judicial Appointments Commissions: The European and North American Experience and the Possible Implications for the United Kingdom* (Lord Chancellor's Department, December 1997).

political background is a legitimate area of enquiry for senior judicial appointments.[62] At the point of selection by the Judicial Appointments Commission, this would be most undesirable: candidates should succeed on the basis of their technical ability, academic brilliance, potential contribution to the diversity of the pool of judges – but not on the basis of their political beliefs or affiliations. An alternative approach would be for a Parliamentary committee to scrutinise newly appointed senior judges before they take office. However, for the time being, this too should be avoided. As Andrew Tyrie MP pointed out to us:

> *"The trouble with select committees is that they are appointed. It is easy for the Government to put placemen on them and control their outcome."*

Whilst the current members of the Constitutional Affairs Select Committee are of a notably high calibre and independent mindset, any strengthening of the Committee's role would undoubtedly provoke the whips to 'doctor' its membership in the future. Therefore, until the issue of government influence over select committees is resolved, committee involvement would seem to bring an even greater threat to judicial independence from the executive than Lord Chancellor under the current system.

Furthermore, it is difficult to see how, if it is to be meaningful, the consideration of individual appointments by a committee of politicians could avoid the politicising the judiciary; incoming senior judges would inevitably be asked to declare their views on contemporary political issues. Yet the very principle underlying the abolition of the Appellate Committee and the Lord Chancellor's judicial functions is to ensure that the judiciary is seen to be *non-political*. Moreover, if judges had to provide answers to political questions before the legislature,

---

62   See *Reform of the Lord Chancellor's Department* (JUSTICE Briefing Paper, June 2003), p.6.

many strong candidates might be put off applying – and so the other key principle of the present reforms, ensuring a meritocratic selection process, may also be compromised.

It would be far better for the Select Committee to scrutinise the Secretary of State's use of his veto and to be presented with an annual report on judicial appointments by the Commission, with an opportunity to question members as to general policy and procedure, but not on individual appointments.

> "I would like to see the Commission accountable to a Parliamentary committee in the sense that it makes an annual report, so that there is a scrutiny at a level of abstraction. And provided that Parliament can provide the resources to monitor that and have a proper hearing, I think that could work very well. Commission members could talk about things such as their aims – for example, to have a younger judiciary, to have a more diverse judiciary. To have a judiciary that is better trained." – **Robin Allen QC**

More generally, we would strongly advocate that meetings of the Judicial Appointments Commission are not held in public, in order to protect the anonymity of rejected candidates. For unsuccessful applicants already in judicial office, open proceedings would undermine their credibility; for practising lawyers, it could have a very damaging effect on their professional reputation. The transparency of the judicial appointments process would be better served by a detailed feedback process and the Commission's presentation of an annual report on its policy and procedure to the Constitutional Affairs Select Committee.

5. The Future of Queen's Counsel

Introduction

Queen's Counsel – commonly referred to as 'silk'[1] – have been appointed in this country since the end of the 16th Century.[2] At the end of 2002, there were 10,742 barristers in England and Wales, of whom 1,145 were Queen's Counsel – around 10%.[3] This is by no means an anomaly: many other countries have a similar system to acknowledge senior advocates. For example, Belize, Hong Kong, India, Ireland, Singapore, South Africa have Senior Counsel; Sri Lanka has President's Counsel; Australia has Senior Counsel in some states and Queen's Counsel in two others;[4] New Zealand and all but two provinces in

---

1   Because of their distinctive court dress.
2   The title becomes 'King's Counsel' under a male monarch.
3   *Constitutional Reform: the Future of Queen's Counsel* (Department for Constitutional Affairs, July 2003), p. 6.
4   The Australian federal Government lacks the power to make appointments. One state declines to exercise the power to appoint.

Canada have a Queen's Counsel system.[5]

In England and Wales, QC appointments have to date been the responsibility of the Lord Chancellor's Department. Applications are invited annually through advertisements placed in September; by tradition, appointments are made on Maundy Thursday.

Written views on the applicants are automatically sought from the judiciary, specialist legal associations and senior practitioners; candidates are invited to nominate six of these whom they feel will know something of their practice to act as referees. They may also put forward six further referees from within the legal profession. In the ensuing consultation process – often called 'secret soundings' – LCD officials hold meetings with senior judges and, where their views need clarification, with candidates' own referees.

Applications are then 'sifted' for evidence that they meet the required standard on the relevant criteria: advocacy ability; legal ability and practice; professional qualities including integrity, professional standing, maturity of judgement and balance.[6] There is no age requirement, but in order to be eligible for consideration, applicants must have been legally qualified for a minimum of ten years. In practice, sucessful candidates tend to have been practising for fifteen to twenty years.

At the end of the sifting process, a 'long list' is produced, containing the names of the candidates whom the Department considers suitable for appointment to silk and explaining the reasons for their inclusion. The Lord Chancellor receives this list, the details of those who were not included on it (with reasons why), and a list of all women, ethnic

---

5.   The Canadian exceptions being Ontario (which stopped making appointments in 1985 but did not repeal its statutory ability to do so) and Quebec (which abolished QC appointments in 1976). The Canadian federal Government ceased making appointments in 1993. At the time of writing, moves are afoot in New Zealand either to reform or to abolish the rank – see Paul Chapman, *New Zealand to Scrap Queen's Counsel Title*, *The Daily Telegraph*, 8th February 2003.

6   *Appointment of Queens Counsel 2003: Guide to Applicants* (Lord Chancellor's Department)

minority, solicitor and regional applicants. He then advises the Queen on appointments. The Lord Chancellor's discretion is entirely unfettered – he is not bound by the long list.

Unsucessful candidates are encouraged to discuss their application with a senior member of the Department: feedback is provided to help understand why they were not successful and they are given a full account of the comments received, edited only so far as necessary to preserve the anonymity of the relevant source.[7]

Challenges to the QC system

In March 2001, the Director General of Fair Trading published a wide-ranging report entitled *Competition in Professions*, which incorporated a much longer report on the legal profession by the Law and Economics Consulting Group commissioned by the Director General.[8] Both these reports criticised many aspects of practice both at the Bar and in the wider legal world, such as rules restricting direct access to barristers, legal professional privilege, restrictions on the formation of multi-disciplinary partnerships, and potential harms of having a divided profession. The reports also – rather briefly – suggested that the silk system constituted a restrictive practice, although they did not explicitly call for its abolition.[9] The Government subsequently released a consultation document, which sought to elicit responses from the legal community on these issues.[10] Once again, the paper was not solely or even largely concerned with the QC system and did not directly question its future. In April 2003, without any warning, Lord Irvine

---

7   Confidentiality is an important part of the comnsultation process. "Lord Mackay suggested that senior members of the profession and the judiciary would be reluctant to give 'sincere and honest' views without the assurance that they were confidential." – Reeves, *Silk Cut: Are Queen's Cunsel necessary?* (Adam Smith Institute, 1998) p. 13.

8   *Competition in Professions* (Director General of Free Trading, March 2001).

9   *Ibid* p. 15.

10   *In the Public Interest? A Consultation Following the Office of Fair Trading's Report on Competition in the Professions* (Lord Chancellor's Department, July 2002).

told new silks at their installation that they might be the last in the line of QCs, announcing that a second consultation paper would be released in July to resolve the matter once and for all.[11] This was released in July 2003, after Lord Irvine's departure from office; drawing on the criticisms presented in response to the first consultation paper, it sets the onus upon those who support the retention of QCs to prove the system's worth.[12]

Arguments for Abolition

Inflating the cost of litigation?

"Many assert that the rank of silk drives up costs unjustifiably." – **Lord Irvine**[13]

Until 1977, the Bar Code of Conduct prohibited Queen's Counsel from appearing in court without one or more 'junior counsel'.[14] Since then, they have been free to do so, but respondents to the Government's first consultation paper suggests that a *de facto* restriction remains in place:[15] for a silk to appear without junior remains rare. Two lawyers obviously cost more than one; therefore, on one view, the QC system inflates the cost of litigation. A second charge is that QCs effectively operate a 'fees cartel', so that they are able to charge more for their fees than they could if the QC system did not exist.

Neither of these arguments is particulary convincing. The onerous nature of modern litigation means that the practice of having multiple

---

11   See Joshua Rozenberg, *This Year's QCs Could Be the Last, Says Lord Irvine, The Daily Telegraph*, 30th April 2003.

12   *Constitutional Reform: The Future of Queen's Counsel* (Department for Constitutional Affairs, July 2003).

13   Speech to newly-installed QCs, 29th April 2003. See Joshua Rozenberg, *This Year's QCs Could Be the Last, Says Lord Irvine, The Daily Telegraph*, 30th April 2003.

14   i.e. barristers who are not QCs.

15   See *Constitutional Reform: the Future of Queen's Counsel* (Department for Constitutional Affairs, July 2003).

barristers representing a client would not diminish upon the abolition of silk; senior barristers – with or without the label 'QC' – will always lead a team of one or more junior barristers. For a 'fees cartel' effectively to operate, QCs would need to have a monopoly over the 'lead' role in cases, so that, in every case requiring more than one barrister, the client would be forced to hire a QC. However, this is not the case: junior barristers are able to lead other juniors, and often do. Consequently, if a QC does not provide value for money, the option is there for clients and solicitors to use a 'leading junior' instead. It would seem, therefore, that market forces already act as a safeguard against silks overcharging their clients. At the very least, the economic case for abolishing QCs is not made out; the LECG's report concedes that its suppositions were not backed up with any "data on fees, profits or earnings". [16]

"If anyone thinks that silks are capable of charging the fees that they do simply because they can put QC after their name they're wrong. There are other reasons for why fees are so high; they charge what the market will let them get away with. People who complain about the fees of silk, have a ready remedy at hand: they can brief a junior barrister." – **Dr Christopher Forsyth**

Transparency of appointments

"I'm very much opposed to the way the system now operates with the secret soundings, and I withdrew from the secret soundings about three years ago, because I found the whole thing arbitrary. You receive a document six inches thick containing hundreds of would-be applicants with their CVs set out, and when you go through it all, you realise that you don't actually know even whether your colleagues in your own chambers are competent to be QCs because you've never appeared with or against them, so you end up supporting a few people you think you know something about, and that's an entirely arbitrary thing." – **Lord Lester of Herne Hill QC**

---

16   *Competition in Professions* (Director General of Free Trading, March 2001), p. 37.

The lack of transparency in the current appointment process for silk is an undeniable problem. It certainly justifies a change to the current system of appointing silks. An end to the unfettered discretion of the Lord Chancellor and a transfer of responsibility for QC selection to the new independent Judicial Appointments Commission would be a positive start.[17] We also agree with Paul Stinchcombe's proposal that applicants should have the opportunity to comment on and rebut negative comments made about them during, before any decision as to appointment is made. However, reforms such as these would substantially neutralise the transparency criticism. Outright abolition of Queen's Counsel is not the only solution.

Unfair on solicitors?

Traditionally, silk could only be awarded to barristers. In 1996, eligibility was extended to solicitors with rights of audience in the 'higher courts'.[18] It has since been claimed that the system remains unfair to solicitors,[19] on the grounds that less than 0.5% of all solicitors are now QCs, compared to 10% of barristers.[20] As a result, the Law Society has recommended the abolition of the Silk system.[21]

However, an equal proportion of silks in both branches of the profession is unrealistic. With its heavy emphasis on advocacy, the QC system was not designed to acknowledge excellence in the traditional work of solicitors, which is to advise clients in non-litigious circumstances and to manage cases that do go to court. The few solicitors who do receive silk, do so in large part because of their

---

17   See p. 152ff..

18   i.e. the Crown Court, the High Court, the Court of Appeal and the House of Lords Appellate Committee.

19   Most notably, by the Law Society, *eg.* in a press release issued on 28th September 1999.

20   In 2002 there were 89,045 solicitors in England and Wales; 1,787 had the right to appear in the higher courts, and of that latter group only seven – less than 0.5% - were Queen's Counsel. See *Constitutional Reform: The Future of Queen's Counsel* (Department for Constitutional Affairs, July 2003), p. 6.

21   The Law Society, press release, 28th September 1999.

advanced skill and experience as advocates – the very field the award is geared to recognise – which remains a rare phenomenon outside of the Bar. No wonder, then, that only seven of the five hundred applicants for the 1997 round of QC selection were solicitors:[22] a recognition that, for the everyday solicitor, the award is irrelevant. The usual goal for solicitors is partnership within their firm, a recognition of ability and experience that has no equivalent at the Bar.

Arguments Against Abolition

A kitemark of quality

> "You need a consultancy rank – the market is not capable of finding the right level. It's exactly the same as consultancy in hospitals. People are entitled to know that the person operating on them or dealing with their case has achieved a certain rank." – **Robert Marshall-Andrews QC MP**

The central question posed during the debate on the future of silk system has been: 'does the existence of the QC rank help the public?' In the immediate sense of facilitating in real terms a definitive or even significant category of barrister more suitable for particular work, the answer must be no. The black and white catagorisation of the QC system is of little use to solicitors in choosing whom to instruct, since it is an important part of their job to evaluate in much greater detail which barristers are suitable for their cases.

However, in our view, the silk system does benefit the public in a wider sense. The existence of a higher rank urges greater performance from those included in it. A silk is benchmarked by a higher standard – that of his fellow QCs, rather than that of barristers generally – and will

---

22   Reeves, *Silk Cut: Are Queen's Counsel Necessary?* (Adam Smith Institute, 1998) p. 13

know that, if he falls short of these greater expectations, his income will plummet. The system may also encourage excellence amongst those who are not yet QCs, spurred on by the prospect of receiving this recognition of professional excellence. As David Pannick QC has recently observed, the promotion of higher standards of advocacy is in the public interest.[23]

Additionally, the rank provides concrete reassurance, to those facing a threat to their liberty and to those seeking to enforce or defend their rights, that their representation in the court is first-class. As in other jurisdictions, it *"provides a public identification of barristers whose standing and achievements justify an expectation, on the part of those who may need their services as well as on the part of the judiciary and the public, that they can provide outstanding services as advocates and advisers, to the good of the administration of justice."*[24] Accordingly, as the Bar Council has recently observed, the QC system promotes public confidence in the law – an important advantage.[25]

"As I sit here now, I would certainly wish to see the silk system preserved. I think it is a genuine mark of quality and is recognised as such by the members of the public who think about it. As far as the market is concerned, the market for the bar is a sophisticated one – solicitors know the barristers very well, as it's a referral profession. On one view that says we don't need the quality mark of silk. But on the other hand, it means that solicitors will recognise that so and so has been given silk and will judge him by a higher standard." – **Lord Justice Laws**

A good way of spotting potential judges

The 'sifting' of candidates for silk is in effect a large information-gathering exercise on leading advocates in their late thirties and forties. Currently and for the foreseeable future, it is from this same group that

---

23   David Pannick QC, The Times, 7 October 2003.
24   Queensland Courts, *Protocol for the Appointment of Senior Counsel and Criteria for Appointments.*
25   *QC Rank Should Be Retained, says Bar* (Bar Council Press Release, July 2003).

the bulk of our judges are drawn. Both appointments processes have until now been the responsibility of the Lord Chancellor's Department; therefore, as Sir Nicholas Lyell QC explained to us, the information gleaned on leading lawyers during the QC selection process has been extremely useful in facilitating the appointment of the most talented candidates to the Bench. This important side-effect of the silk system need not be discarded if judicial appointments are in future to be controlled by an independent commission; as discussed below, that commission could – and should – assume responsibility for appointing silks as well.[26]

A critical message given to other countries

A result of Britain's imperial past is the existence of common-law jurisdictions throughout the globe. Many of these jurisdictions have a two-tier ranking system similar to our own.[27] In abolishing our higher rank, we are implicitly suggesting that theirs – many of which acknowledge our Queen – is wrong, when the majority of them appear to consider the approach to be entirely satisfactory.[28] Whilst not a decisive point, the government's failure to consult these countries as to their thoughts on the rank of silk at the very least seems discourteous.

> "One of the things I found objectively quite crude about the proposals to abolish the QC system was this: it seems offensive simply to say that QCs ought to be reviewed, without asking the other countries that have silk. Because it seems to say if they're under threat here, they should be there, too. It seemed to me they haven't really asked themselves why other countries have adopted the system." – **Michael Beloff QC**

26   See p. 152ff.
27   See p.141.
28   A notable exception is New Zealand, where there have been calls to abolish the rank – see Paul Chapman, *New Zealand to Scrap Queen's Counsel Title*, *The Daily Telegraph*, 8th February 2003.

Enforcing the change

If the Government were to abolish the Queen's Counsel, it is quite likely that the Bar Council, which opposes abolition,[29] would set up its own 'Senior Counsel' award for recognising senior barristers. Yet such a system would be just as offensive to those who oppose QCs, and would not retain all of the benefits of the status quo – for example, the valuable information network gathered in the process of appointing QCs would be unavailable to those appointing judges. Moreover, the endorsement of barristers by the barristers' union would inevitably appear even less transparent and even more 'cliquey' than the current system. If run solely by the Bar Council,[30] *no* solicitors – not even the most talented solicitor-advocates – could become QCs.

Of course, the Government could sponsor legislation preventing a private 'Senior Counsel' system, but that in itself would be a highly authoritarian move. Equally authoritarian would be steps needed to enforce a complete and effective abolition of the present QC system. If existing silks are allowed to retain their title – or even if they are allowed to publicise that they were formerly QCs – the complaints that silk enables barristers to charge excessive fees would (if they were valid in the first place) still stand unresolved. The only difference would be that the ladder would be pulled up under the feet of the existing silks, so that nobody else could enter their 'privileged rank' – surely an even more objectionable scenario! Yet for such an outcome to be avoided, there would have to be a ban on these barristers referring to their former title. Such a prohibition would be a huge inroad into their freedom of expression; so much so that a challenge under the Human Rights Act 1998, invoking Article 10

---

29   *QC Rank Should Be Retained, says Bar* (Bar Council Press Release, July 2003).
30   As would no doubt be the case, since the Law Society support the abolition of silk.

of the European Convention on Human Rights, may well prove successful.[31]

Summary: Why Queen's Counsel Should Be Retained

As the foregoing suggests, the rank of Queen's Counsel has its virtues and there are some very difficult practical obstacles to its complete and effective abolition. Whilst it may be the case that none of these provides a 'knockout' argument in favour of retaining QCs, the case for abolition is not made out at all. The economic criticisms of the silk system are factually unsubstantiated and theoretically unconvincing; other criticisms either have no weight or simply justify a change to the current method of appointment rather than outright abolition. Therefore, for the time being at least, the balance hangs clearly in favour of the retentionists.

Pointedly, it would appear that the Government has attempted to rig this balance by insisting – contrary to standard practice – that it was for proponents of the status quo to justify present arrangements, rather than for critics to present a convincing case for abolition. To quote Lord Justice Laws:

"If you're going to abolish a very long established public institution – the silk system has been in existence (with changes of course) for three or four hundred years – the burden of proof, to use a legalistic term, is very much on the abolitionists. Lord Falconer said that it will be up to the Bar or the legal profession to justify retention – I was rather nonplussed by this reversal of the burden."

---

31 Although, of course, this could not result in an Act of Parliament being overturned; rather, the Court would, in such a situation, issue a 'declaration of incompatibility' in accordance with Section 4 of the Human Rights Act 1998.

The most likely reason for the burden of proof being switched in this manner is that the Government has already decided to abolish silk and the consultation process is merely a smokescreen. In its present time of crisis, and faced with its failures in other areas of constitutional reform (most notably, the House of Lords), the Government may well be seeking to use the abolition of QCs to claim plaudits for 'modernisation' and 'bold reform'.

> "Getting rid of it is an exercise in cheap populism, and intended to sweeten or obscure other parts of the package of reform and present this as some kind of consumer protection measure." – **Professor Ian Loveland**

Ending the Executive's Patronage

Whilst supporting the retention of Queen's Counsel, we recommend one crucial change to the current system of appointments to silk: the removal of the executive's input.

As already discussed in Chapters Three and Four, in recent decades, the office of Lord Chancellor has become increasingly 'political', the incumbents prioritising their executive and party-political responsibilities over their duty to act as an impartial head of the judiciary.[32] This has important implications not only for the Lord Chancellor's judicial functions, but also for his role in appointing QCs, as vividly seen in 2001, when Lord Irvine *"faced calls for his resignation… after he admitted asking lawyers who depend on him for their promotions to give money to the Labour Party"* at fundraising dinners and in letters.[33] Many of his addressees were potential candidates for appointment as QCs. His unapologetic response was: *"it is not the case that the Lord Chancellor is not party political"*[34] – which hardly

---

32   See p.88ff.
33   Benedict Brogan, *Irvine in Funds for Jobs Row, The Daily Telegraph*, 19th February 2001.
34   *ibid.*

dispelled onlookers' fears that political considerations enter into the appointments process.

The Lord Chancellor's absolute discretion over appointments to silk can only damage the effectiveness of the QC label as a recognition of extreme merit, in the eyes of both legal professionals and the general public. This is particularly important given the fact that many of these QCs will ultimately become judges. Just as a Cabinet Minister should no longer hold the initiative for the appointment of new judges,[35] he should not have patronage over the judges of the future either – especially since the intervening time between appointment to silk and appointment to the Bench is well within the potential lifespan of a government.

Accordingly, we propose that the selection of QCs should be the responsibility of the Judicial Appointments Commission rather than a Cabinet Minister. The Commission would put forward a list of appointments to the Secretary of State for Constitutional Affairs, leaving him with no choice or veto; he would then formally recommend them to the Queen.[36] Such a model would present a neat symmetry of transferral of responsibility from the Government to an independent body for appointments both to the Bench and to silk. As discussed above, controlling both in the same place means that those appointing judges are able to use QC selection as an invaluable 'talent-spotting' process. Of course, the Commission would hardly be involved in the lengthy sifting process, just as the Lord Chancellor hardly scrutinises each individual QC candidate now.[37] The benefit comes rather from the common pooling of information in those who do carry out the process on a day-to-day basis: the civil servants. The Commission should retain an absolute discretion as to appointments – so that, like

---

35   See pp. 117–119.

36   The need for a minister make the formal recommendation to the Queen for Crown Appointments is explained at pp. 120–121

37   See p.122, n.20.

the Lord Chancellor before it, it may select a candidate who is not included on the long list presented to it – in order to prevent 'faceless civil servants' from having the last word on any candidate's application. However, the fact that this discretion would be exercised by an independent committee rather than a party-political Cabinet Minister may go a long way to answering criticisms that the present QC appointments system lacks transparency.

Bibliography

Bagehot, *The English Constitution* (Kegan, Paul & Co, 1905)

Bean (ed.) *Law Reform for All* (Blackstone Press, 1996)

Bradley and Ewing, *Constitutional and Administrative Law* (13th Edn., Longman, 2003)

Cornes, *McGonnell v United Kingdom, the Lord Chancellor and the Law Lords* (2000) *Public Law* p.166; *The Supreme Court of the United Kingdom* (2003) *New Law Journal* vol.153, p.1018; *Constitutional Reform: A Supreme Court for the United Kingdom* (forthcoming article)

Craig, *Formal and Substantive Conceptions of the Rule of Law* (1997) *Public Law* p.467

Lord Denning, *What Next in the Law* (Butterworths, 1982)

Dicey, *An Introduction to the Study of the Law of the Constitution* (10th Edn., Macmillan Press, 1975)

Garnier, *Good Riddance? The Office of the Lord Chancellor: What is the Government Up To, and Do We Care?, Counsel,* July 2003

Genn, *Paths to Justice: What People Do and Think about Going to Law* (Hart Publishing, 1999)

Glazebrook, *Still No Code!* in Dockray (ed.), City University Centenary Lectures in Law (Blackstone Press, 1996)

Gordon and Wilmot-Smith (eds.) *Human Rights in the United Kingdom* (Oxford University Press, 1996)

Lord Hailsham of St Marylebone LC, *The Dilemma of Democracy: Diagnosis and Prescription* (Collins, 1978); *The Office of Lord Chancellor and the Separation of Powers* (1989) *Civil Justice Quarterly* vol. 8, p.308

Harrison, *What Pinochet Has Done for the Law Lords* (1999) *New Law Journal* vol. 149, p.477

Harvey and Bather *The British Constitution* (2nd Edn., Macmillan, 1968)

Hazell, *Separating Powers, Prospect,* August 2003, pp.10-11

Jowell and Oliver (eds.), *The Changing Constitution* (3rd Edn., Clarendon Press, 1994)

Kentridge *The Highest Court: Selecting the Judges* (2003) *Cambridge Law Journal* vol. 62, p.55

Legg, *Judges for the New Century* (2001) *Public Law,* p.74

Le Sueur and Cornes, *The Future of the United Kingdom's Highest Courts* (The Constitution Unit, 2001)

Loveland, *Constitutional Law* (2nd Edn., Butterworths, 2000)

Lord Mackay, *The Lord Chancellor in the 1990s* (1991) *Current Legal Problems,* vol. 44, p.241

Malleson, *The Legal System* (Butterworths, 2003); *Justifying Gender Equality on the Bench: Why Difference Won't Do* (2003) *Feminist Legal Studies* vol.11, p.1

McAulsan and McEldowney (eds.), *Law, Legitimacy and the Constitution* (Sweet and Maxwell, 1985)

Megarry, *Lawyer and Litigant in England* (Stevens & Sons, 1962)

Mole and Harby, *The Right to a Fair Trial: A Guide to the Implementation of Article 6 of the European Convention on Human Rights* (Council of Europe, 2001)

Pannick, *Judges* (Oxford University Press, 1998)

Peter Reeves, *Silk Cut: Are Queen's Counsel Necessary?* (Adam Smith Institute, 1998)

Russell and Cornes, *The Royal Commission on Reform of the House of Lords: a House for the Future?* (2001) *Modern Law Review* vol.82, p.92.

Skordaki, *Judicial Appointments: An international review of existing models* (The Law Society, 1991)

Spencer, *Time for a Ministry of Justice?* (Institute for Public Policy Research, 2001)

Stevens, *The Independence of the Judiciary* (Clarendon Press, 1997)

Lord Steyn, *The Weakest and Least Dangerous Department of Government* (1997) *Public* Law, p.84; *The Case for a Supreme Court* (2002) *Law Quarterly Review* vol. 118, p.382

Thomas and Malleson, *Judicial Appointments Commissions: The European and North American Experience and the Possible Implications for the United Kingdom* (Lord Chancellor's Department, 1997)

Tyrie, *The Chancellor's Department: Time to Go* (December 2002, unpublished)

Underhill, *The Lord Chancellor* (Terence Dalton, 1978)

Wade and Forsyth, *Administrative Law* (8th Edn., Oxford University Press, 2000)

Wade, *The Basis of Legal Sovereignty* (1955) *Cambridge Law Journal* p.172

Woodhouse *The Office of the Lord Chancellor* (Hart Publishing, 2001)

News Articles and Commment

Lord Alexander of Weedon, *Is this a ruthless grab for power?*, *The Times*, 1st July 2003

Benedict Brogan, *Irvine in Funds for Jobs Row*, *The Daily Telegraph* 19th February 2001

Paul Chapman, *New Zealand to Scrap Queen's Counsel Title*, *The Daily Telegraph*, 8th February 2003

Clare Dyer, *Top Judges 'Face Being Gagged'*, *The Guardian*, 16th September 2003

Frances Gibb, *More Judges Needed For Rights Challenges*, *The Times*, 7th September 1999, Irvine *Can't be a Judge, says Human Rights Report*, *The Times*, 3rd March 2003; *Judicial Integrity Must be Preserved, says Woolf*, *The Times*, 10th July 2003; *Closing the Silk Route Is Not a 'Done Deal'*, *The Times*, 23rd September 2003

George Jones, *Irvine 'To Go in Summer Reshuffle'*, *The Daily Telegraph*, 5th June 2003

Daniel Lightman and Stanley Brodie, *Treading the Line between Law Lord and Politician*, *The Times* Tuesday 4th March 2003

William Rees-Mogg, *The Supreme Court; Isn't There Some Law Against It?*, *The Times* 4th August 2003

Joshua Rozenberg, *Lord Falconer's Court May Not Be So Supreme*, *The Daily Telegraph*, 26th June 2003; *This Year's QCs Could Be the Last, Says Lord Irvine*, *Daily Telegraph*, 30th April 2003; The *Bar Fights to Keep its Own Counsel*, *The Daily Telegraph*, 18th September 2003

Rachel Sylvester, *Irvine Withdraws from Sitting as a Judge in the Lords*, *The Daily Telegraph*, 21st February 2001

Patrick Wintour and Claire Dyer, *Ministers Shun US Model for Supreme Court*, *The Guardian*, 16th June 2003

Patrick Wintour and Nicholas Wyatt, *PM Endorses Irvine on Lords*, *The Guardian*, 30th January 2002; *Blunkett Fights Off Ministry of Justice Plan*, *The Guardian*, 12th June 2003.

Hugo Young, *Irvine was Power Hungry, But He Stood up for Judges*, *The Guardian* 17th June 2003

Public Lectures

Lord Bingham of Cornhill, *The Evolving Constitution*, lecture to

JUSTICE, October 2001; *A New Supreme Court for the UK*, lecture to The Constitution Unit, May 2002

Lord Falconer of Thoroton, Address to HM Judges, Mansion House, 9th July 2003

Lord Irvine of Lairg, Address to HM Judges, Mansion House, 23rd July 1997

Reports / Press Releases / Briefing Papers

American Bar Association Standing Committee on Judicial Independence *Standards on State Judicial Selection* (July 2000)

Bar Council Working Party on Judicial Appointments and Silk (Bar Council Consultation Document, March 2003)

QC Rank Should Be Retained, says Bar (Bar Council Press Release, July 2003)

Judicial Functions of the House of Lords, (JUSTICE, written evidence to the Royal Commission on the Reform of the House of Lords, May 1999)

A Supreme Court for the United Kingdom (JUSTICE Policy Paper, November 2002)

A Supreme Court for the United Kingdom (JUSTICE Briefing Paper, May 2003)

Sir Leonard Peach *Independent Scrutiny of the Appointment Processes of Judges and Queen's Counsel* (December 1999)

Queensland Courts *Protocol for the Appointment of Senior Counsel and Criteria for Appointment*.

Governmental Publications

A House for the Future. Royal Commission on the Reform of the House of Lords, Cm. 4534 (January 2000)

Department for Constitutional Affairs, *Constitutional Reform: the Future of Queen's Counsel*, CP 08/03 (July 2003)

Department for Constitutional Affairs, *Constitutional Reform: A New Way of Appointing Judges*, CP 10/03 (July 2003)

Department for Constitutional Affairs, *Constitutional Reform: a Supreme Court for the United Kingdom*, CP 11/03 (July 2003)

Department for Constitutional Affairs, *Constitutional Reform: Reforming the Office of the Lord Chancellor*, CP 13/03 (July 2003)

Director General of Free Trading, *Competition in Professions* (March 2001)

The Lord Chancellor's Department, *Judicial Appointments* (February 2003)

The Lord Chancellor's Department, *Judicial Statistics*

The Lord Chancellor's Department, *Modernising Justice: The Government's Plans for Reforming Legal Services and the Courts* (December 1998).

The Lord Chancellor's Department, *Appointment of Queen's Counsel 2003: Guide for Applicants* (2003)

The Lord Chancellor's Department *In the Public Interest? A Consultation following the Office of Fair Trading's report on Competition in the Professions* (July 2002)

Abbreviations Commonly Used

A.C. – Appeal Cases (Law Reports)
C.L.J. – Cambridge Law Journal
E.H.R.R. – European Human Rights Reports
L.Q.R. – Law Quarterly Review
M.L.R. – Modern Law Review
P.L. – Public Law
W.L.R. – Weekly Law Reports

About Policy Exchange

Policy Exchange is an independent think tank whose mission is to develop and promote new policy ideas which will foster a free society based on limited government, strong communities, personal freedom and national self-confidence.

Working in partnership with independent academics and experts, we commission original research into important issues of policy and use the findings to develop practical recommendations for government. Policy Exchange seeks to learn lessons from the approaches adopted in other countries and to assess their relevance to the UK context. We aim to engage with people and groups across the political spectrum and not be restricted by outdated notions of left and right.

Policy Exchange is a registered charity (no: 1096300) and is funded by individuals, grant-making trusts and companies.

essays in political and cultural criticism

Contemporary public debate has been impoverished by two competing trends. On the one hand the increasing commercialisation of the visual media has meant that in-depth commentary has given way to the ten-second soundbite. On the other hand the explosion of scholarly knowledge has led to such a degree of specialisation that academic discourse has ceased to be comprehensible. As a result writing on politics and culture tends to be either superficial or baffling.

This was not always so—especially in the field of politics. The high point of the English political pamphlet was the seventeenth century, when a number of small printer-publishers responded to the political ferment of the age with an outpouring of widely-accessible pamphlets and tracts. Indeed Imprint Academic operates a reprint service under the banner of 'The Rota', offering facsimile editions of works such as *The World's Mistake in Oliver Cromwell*.

In recent years the tradition of the political pamphlet has declined—with most publishers rejecting anything under 100,000 words as uneconomic. The result is that many a good idea has ended up drowning in a sea of verbosity. However the introduction of the digital press makes it possible to re-create a more exciting age of publishing. *Societas* authors are all experts in their own field, either scholarly or professional, but the essays are aimed at a general audience. Each book should take no more than an evening to read.

The books are available through the retail trade at the price of £8.95/$14.95 each, or on bi-monthly subscription for only £5.00/$8.50. Subscribers may purchase back volumes for only £2.50/$4.25 each. Full details and forthcoming title information from Imprint Academic: **www.imprint-academic.com/societas**

IMPRINT ACADEMIC, PO Box 200, Exeter, EX5 5YX, UK
Tel: **(0)1392 841600** Fax: **(0)1392 841478** Email: **sandra@imprint.co.uk**

SOCIETAS

Democracy, Fascism and the New World Order
Ivo Mosley

Growing up as the grandson of the 1930s blackshirt leader, made Ivo Mosley consider fascism with a deep interest. Whereas conventional wisdom sets up democracy and fascism as opposites, to ancient political theorists democracy had an innate tendency to lead to extreme populist government, and provided demagogues with the opportunity to seize power. This book argues that totalitarian regimes can be the outcome of unfettered mass democracy.

SOCIETAS   96 pp., £8.95/$14.95, 0907845 649

The Liberty Option
Tibor R. Machan

The Liberty Option advances the idea that for compelling moral and practical reasons it is the society organised on classical liberal principles that serves justice best, leads to prosperity and encourages the greatest measure of individual virtue. The book contrasts the Lockean ideal with the various statist alternatives, defends it against its communitarian critics and lays out some of its more significant policy implications. Machan is a research fellow at Stanford University's Hoover Institution. He has written extensively on classical liberal theory, including *Classical Individualism* (Routledge, 1998).

SOCIETAS   104 pp., £8.95/$14.95, 0907845 630

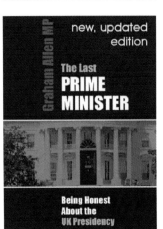

The Last Prime Minister
Graham Allen MP

Echoing Gandhi's comment on Western civilization, Graham Allen thinks the British constitution would be a very good idea. In *The Last Prime Minister* he showed the British people how they had acquired an executive presidency by stealth. This timely new edition takes in new issues, including Parliament's constitutional impotence over Iraq.

'Sharp, well-informed and truly alarming.' **Peter Hennessy**
'Iconoclastic, stimulating and well-argued, it's publication could hardly be more timely.' **Vernon Bogdanor, THES**

SOCIETAS   96 pp. £8.95/$14.95 0907845 41X

sample chapters, reviews and TOCs: www.imprint-academic.com/societas

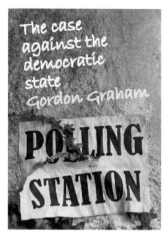

The Case Against the Democratic State

Gordon Graham

We are now so used to the state's pre-eminence in all things that few think to question it. This essay contends that the gross imbalance of power in the modern state is in need of justification, and that democracy simply masks this need with an illusion of popular sovereigny. Although the arguments are accessible to all, it is written within the European philosophical tradition. The author is Professor of Moral Philosophy at the Uniiversity of Aberdeen.

SOCIETAS   96 pp., £8.95/$14.95, 0907845 38X

The Party's Over

Keith Sutherland

The UK political party started as a loose association of like-minded MPs. However, in recent years the tail has been wagging the dog—politicians now have no choice but to whip themselves into line behind a strong leader with the essential televisual charisma. This book outlines the reasons behind the changes in modern politics and questions the role of the party in the post-ideological age. If we are now all middle-class and share the liberal capitalist consensus, then what is the point of the political party? The book concludes that we should re-interpret our constitutional monarchy more literally.

SOCIETAS   96 pp., £8.95/$14.95, 0907845 517

The Modernization Imperative

Bruce Charlton & Peter Andras

Modernisation gets a bad press in the UK, and is blamed for the dumbing down of public life. But modernisation is preferable to lapsing back towards a static, hierarchical society. The many criticisms of modernisation should be seen as specific problems relating to a process that is broadly beneficial. This book explains the importance of modernisation to all societies and analyses anti-modernisation in the UK—especially such problems as class divisions, political short-termism and the culture of spin.

SOCIETAS   96 pp., £8.95/$14.95, 0907845 525

Universities:
The Recovery of an Idea

Gordon Graham

The conclusion of this meditation on Cardinal Newman's classic *The Idea of a University* is that universities should be liberated from state control.

'Those who care about universities should thank Gordon Graham for doing what has needed doing so urgently'.
Philosophy

'Though densely and cogently argued, this book is extremely readable and deserves to be widely read'.
Philosophical Quarterly

136 pp., £8.95, 0907845 371

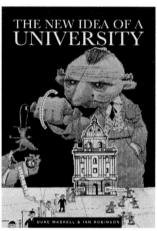

The New Idea of a University

Duke Maskell and Ian Robinson

The New Idea of a University is an entertaining and highly readable defence of the philosophy of liberal arts education and an attack on the sham that has been substituted for it. It will scandalize the friends of the establishment and be cheered elsewhere.

'Seminal text in the battle to save quality education'. **THES**
'A wonderful book'. **Chris Woodhead, Sunday Telegraph**
'A severe indictment of our universities'. **Oxford Magazine**
'The single most important essay on the university system in the past twenty years'. **Cambridge Quarterly**

208 pp., £12.95, 0907845 347

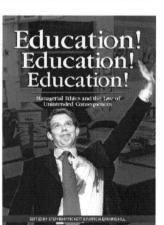

Education! Education! Education!

Edited by Stephen Prickett

The essays in this book criticise the new positivism in education policy, whereby education is systematically reduced to those things that can be measured by so-called 'objective' tests. Contributors include Libby Purves, Evan Harris, Archbishop Rowan Williams, Roger Scruton, Robert Grant, Bruce Charlton and Anthony Smith.

'This book is a call for discernment . . . and finally it is a call to action.' **Dom Antony Sutch, The Tablet**

200 pp., £14.95, 0907845 363

sample chapters, reviews and TOCs: **www.imprint-academic.com**